Perfectly Imperfect

A Story of The Process Of Forgiveness

Kimberly Fairley

Perfectly Imperfect; A Story of the Process of Forgiveness
Copyright © March 2014
By Kimberly Farley

Published in the United States of America by
ChosenButterflyPublishing, LLC

www.cb-publishing.com

ISBN:978-0-9915202-2-0
First Edition Printing
Printed In the United States of America
April 2014

All rights reserved under International Copyright Law. Contents and/or cover may not be reproduced, distributed, or transmitted in any form or by any means or stored in a database or retrieval system, without the prior, written consent of the publisher and/or author.

All scriptures were used from:
Crossway Bibles. English Standard Version Study Bible. Wheaton, Illinois: Good News Publishers, 2007. www.crosswaybibles.com

Heroes For Sale lyrics: Andy Mineo. Heroes For Sale. Reach Records, 2013.
www.andymineo.com
www.reachrecords.com

Forgiveness is not always easy, but accepting it makes life a lot easier than when we submit to the lack of forgiveness - birthing a lifestyle of bitterness.

Special Thanks

Saundra Womack

Thank you for being the best mom I could ask for. Thank you for loving me in spite of my craziness.

Jimmie & Jada Redman

When I told you about my desire to finish my book you believed in my story when I no longer believed in myself. Giving me the computer to finish this book was an act of pure and crazy love and confidence. THANK YOU

Daniel Settlemire

YOU FIXED MY COMPUTER!!!!!! Thank you so much for helping me get this finished.

Darnica Gordon

Co-Founder and Editor

Christ it Up Magazine

You believed in me and my testimony. Thank you for your time.

Rick & Natalie Paladin
& Word & Worship

Some of the greatest leaders one could ever ask for. Your love surpasses anything I have ever known on this side of Heaven. It blows my mind to see the way you have shaped and molded the ministry and how things just trickle from the leadership down. You two loved on me in a tough time and made it easy for me to move forward and not be scared to grow or be successful in Christ.
THANK YOU

Laura, Keonna, Elisha, Alex, & Chakarian

For loving me in spite of me! For being there in one of the toughest periods in my life. For looking past what I had been through and lifting me up. For supporting me at times when I did not know how to support myself. For very simply loving me. Thank you for being a true friend.

Where it all Began

When we are young, we all have a sense of hope, the confident expectation in our futures. Hope that when we get older we may graduate from high school, go to college, get married, have children - or even become doctors, famous musicians, actors and the like. This hope keeps us alive and motivates us throughout our childhood and teenage years. That is until that hope is tainted by the influences of our peers, family, life's experiences, or the world we live in.

When our hope is pure, we believe that even the most impossible things can be achieved. Kind of like the child-like faith that is so pure and innocent. It is not until we leave the covering of our parents or guardians that we begin to experience life for what it really is and many times, it can be while we are under their covering - or a lack there of, that we begin to see the different struggles that come along with this experience called life. Things that we never knew existed, due to the love our parents and guardians had for us and protected us from being able to see.

When I was growing up, the confident expectation I had for my future was that I was going to be my mother's first child of six to both graduate from high school, then college, then get married and have children. I was excited to do life in exactly that order because that is what I perceived as being the "right way" to go through life; the one way that people would be proud of me and without shame. The passion that drove me as a child was that I always wanted to make my mother proud and outside of that, I always wanted to do things according to what the world saw as being proper. I wanted to do things by the book. I wanted to remain abstinent until marriage and then have children, but only after finishing college first to ensure I had a decent job to help provide for my family. I mean in my head this all appeared to be more than the right way to carry myself.

I had grown up with that clear and reasonable understanding of what I wanted for myself. Little had I known that there was a generational seed that had been planted in my life long before I was born; a seed that would one day grow into the ugliest and most overbearing monkey on my back - one that would eventually lead me to believe that even my own death was more desirable than the desire to live.

I was born September 26, 1986 just three minutes before my twin brother (of whom no one, including the doctors and my mother ever knew existed until he was born!). In total my mother raised six children; four boys and two girls by herself. There is my (only) sister (on my mom's side) who we call Tony, my oldest brother we call Jr, my older brother Greg (and my favorite big brother only because we are extremely close and he is one of my biggest supporters), then my twin brother Kendall and I - and last but certainly not least, my favorite baby brother David.

When I was of age, my mother had told my twin brother and me the story of our birth. It was something I was more than interested in learning about. See for as long as I could remember, there was never a "man" of the house. For some time it appeared to be the norm and I was ok with that, but when I became school-aged, it really started to bother me. I wanted to be like the other kids; the kids who on holidays had their parents come in to help with activities and so on. So when we were able to understand (around the age of 10) she told us that when we were born my father came into the room - looked at us, said he was going to the store and never came back and that was simply it.

There was not another appearance from him in our lives, not for holidays, birthdays - nothing. This always troubled me after I heard this. I was just confused. I mean who does that. Why would he do it?

After hearing this, growing up I always felt like an odd ball. In grade school, I always wondered why I could not be like the other children. I mean why was I not worthy of the same things they had? Other children had their parents come in for "bring your dad to school day", to participate during holiday activities, even to be taken to their parents' place of work and here I was stuck looking at the other kids have fun. I would sit and look at the smiles on their faces, as they were so happy and proud of their fathers. Why was I not able to have my father too? Why was my family incomplete?

Knowing that my dad left and never came back planted a deep-rooted seed of loneliness and unworthiness that had begun to grow inside of me. As a young girl I never thought I was pretty. I never had a dad to tell me how beautiful I was, to hold me close, to tell me I was his little princess, or protect me as a father does. This was the heaviest dark cloud that always hovered over me as I was growing up. I never felt good enough. I know my mother loved me, but I was never really encouraged that I was beautiful. Those words were so foreign to me, that when I did finally hear them - they were words that were used against me and not to better how I felt about myself. They were used not as a means to encourage me, but to break down my walls of defense and to infiltrate the innocence I once had.

My brothers never really protected me or encouraged me either. Now I want to stop to say I have the best mom and brothers in the entire world - but because of not having a father figure, they never knew how to cover or protect me. I was picked on a lot, which is something that all little sisters (or siblings in general) just endure. It is almost like your initiation into the family!

To make matters worse, my mom used to dress me in some of the most ridiculous outfits, now that I think back to what I used to look like when I was coming up. I remember days when my mom could not do my hair because of pain she had in her hands, so I was left to fend for myself at times. My hair used to look wicked to say the least. Raggedy attempts at ponytails and so on. Now by all means my mother did her very best to provide for us, so in no way am I trying to discredit anything that she has done for me - but I mean come on, did I have to look like raggedy Anne too! I did not have much going for me to begin with and having a lack of the current and hip things in life at that time, did not make life any easier for me.

Until the age of thirteen, I was purely 'mama's baby and daddy's maybe' (well technically, I was not his 'maybe' because he did not want me from what I had known). I did any and everything for my mother. No matter what she needed, I was there for my mom. I would run to her beckoning call if she needed help putting on her shoes or find something she lost - and let me tell you I was the absolute QUEEN at finding my mother's lost things. It was as if she would say what it was and then just minutes later I had recovered it for her. This brought me so much joy because she always bragged about me as a result of this. I loved her more than anything and she was all I knew. I would do anything in the world for her.

My childhood was not the greatest with the greatest things in it, but it was a good one in the fact that I was safe, loved and well cared for. It was around the age of thirteen that I remember getting into trouble. I mean I had done a decent share of shady things, but it was at this time that really changed my life and how I operated.

See my mother was a hands-on parent (and by all means I think it was a blessing, although at the time I was not a fan). If I ever got into trouble - depending on the severity of the crime, I either got a beating or some form of punishment such as running in place or standing in the corner on my head (yes it was just as terrible as it sounds!). My mother was never the parent to let things go so easy. I remember doing something wrong in the neighborhood we lived in at the time; it got back to mom, then my mother put me in the corner and laid down for a nap. Now when we were put in the corner, we were to either stand up straight with our face straight in the corner and hands to our sides, or we were to stand on our heads (either way it was done it was still terrible!). Now when I was younger (although I am not proud of this), there were times when I was mad at my mother and would say things so that she would clearly know how I felt. I wanted her to hurt just as much as I was hurting. You know even to this day, my mom still tells me how powerful my words are. It was like I was on a quest to use my words in the most powerful way possible and sadly over the years, I grew to use them to really hurt people. I knew I was really good at it (even without having to curse).

Now back to this discipline concept that our world knows nothing of in this present day. When I was coming up being disciplined physically was not a crime at all. I mean your parents were not in fear of having the police come knocking at their door if they followed the saying 'to spare the rod, spoil the child', but one thing my mom did quite often outside of beating us, was to make us stand in the corner. It was the worst. Standing in the corner for HOURS just looking at the wall. I mean who enjoys doing that?

Man it was so cruel and just plain old ungodly parental behavior. Now there was one incident in which I had kind of been the neighborhood terror. Mom put me in the corner (among too many to count) - I waited some time, but I began to cry, "I want my daddy." Now for any single mother (no matter how strong you think you are) this would hurt to know that you have spent years raising your child by yourself (although you had not created the child by yourself), just for your child to proclaim that they would much rather be around the one who had not made the same sacrifices you had. For some reason in the back of my head, I really thought that proclaiming this statement would do me some justice. I was convinced, but oh boy – I did not think this through very well.

See I was not thinking of hurting my mother at this time. No, I simply wanted to excuse this dreaded punishment I was to endure for who knew how long. I was not sure what justice this would do for me, but anything would help to get me out of this misery. Little had I known that my world was about to change drastically.

Again, while I was standing in the corner for what appeared to be an eternity, I declared loud enough for my mother to hear while she was laying down, "I want my daddy" (and this was stated several times). In a matter of minutes, my opinion of him changed. I remember my mother beating the snot out of me. Sometime after this incident all I could think was "I can't believe I just took a beating for a man who doesn't even love me".

From that point forward, I had vowed to myself that this man no longer existed or even mattered. For the longest time that was the easiest concept to accept - but the hard thing about having a twin is that often times our personalities and opinions on matters like this can be the complete opposite and often times very confrontational. See before this incident, my twin brother and I had the strongest wish and desire to find and meet our father. There were many times when we would skip the opportunity to be kids and have fun, just to wait around for disappointment.

One time in particular was right after the beating took place. I was around 11 years old and my brothers and I were a part of the Salvation Army. We did all the activities, including the summer activities such as Vacation Bible School. It was my favorite.

I mean truly we had become the poster kids for the Salvation Army. One summer (I am not sure what the activity was), we had gotten that call that we would get to meet our dad. Even though I was mad, I was still a little hopeful. All I could think was, "man could this be it?!?" Well although hopeful, we waited around the house missing out on all the fun, just to be disappointed yet again. In spite of this disappointment my brother remained hopeful - but after that beating, I was no longer a very big fan of this man.

My brother had maintained his hope of meeting our father and tried his best to make me see things from his point of view. This would be the basis of many arguments for my twin brother and me throughout most of our lives. One of my character flaws is that once someone gets on my bad or dark side, there is very little hope for them to ever be redeemed. To this day I have gotten better, but this is something I do tend to struggle with.

So now, I was stuck with the feelings of being inadequate in my own skin and hatred for the man who had made me feel that way. While growing up I did not know that hating my dad for walking away, would eventually poison me all the way down to my soul. As I grew up, the seed of inadequacy had begun to slowly grow. I never once thought I was pretty. I was a black little girl with no father, a single overworked mother, siblings that had not grasped the concept of love, nappy hair, low self-esteem and self-worth. For years I tried to gain the approval of my mother. I did not know what else to do, so when she called I ran to the rescue. No matter what she needed, I was there. Now the bible does tell us to honor our mother and father that our days shall be long - but I depended so heavily on the approval of my mom that when our relationship made a turn for the worst, I made the decision to walk on the wild side. Around 13 was the time that I became very rude, mouthy, mean, and any other word that can be used to describe a mean person. As a side note, I am not sure what it is about the age of 13. I do not think it happens to every single kid, but that is such a dark time in the life of a teen.

So at 13 I was the 'Grinch' all year with my family, but I made it a point to be nice to those who weren't related to me because I figured their impression of me was far more important than the people I lived with. Among many nicknames I've had during the course of life due to my choice to be so rude, were 'Evilina' and 'Emily Rose' (yes from the Exorcism). I had developed this persona of not caring about anyone around me. I would say the most hurtful things and I did not care who I said them to. I have even made my mother cry on many occasions and I have deeply offended my twin brother and so many others over the course of my life. At the time, I had not realized or even known that hurt people will hurt people. I had not realized that it was not who God had created me to be, but more of whom I turned into as a result of life - but this is no excuse to allow our circumstances to negatively impact our behaviors.

So for years I walked in and out of relationships. I had offended so many people, but for some reason I just had not cared. Over time my heart began to grow cold and hard as a rock - but I could never tell because it was still beating, so to me I was ok. I felt as though I needed to be tough on the outside because I did not see what else I had going for myself. Slowly, I had also lost the concept of what it was to truly love and the need to forgive. Why should I love these people? What was the point in loving myself if my own father could look at me as just a baby and walk away with not a single bit of concern or regret?

On several occasions, due to the extreme lack of self-esteem and self-worth I had for myself, I tried to commit suicide. I am not proud when I say this, but I remember one time in particular I was upset for some reason (I truly seemed to stay upset - maybe to seek attention, who knows). In one of the houses we lived in my mom had this huge cabinet. It was like a mobile metal closet that at one point we colored purple. When I would get lonely or upset I would take my covers and sleep in the bottom of it. Now it was not the most comfortable thing to do, but it satisfied me.

Many times my family members could not find me (until they caught on to what I was doing and then I just became a weirdo) and that made me feel good, because then I had people that were looking for me. At that point, it just felt like people cared, which is something I had not experienced too often. This one evening I felt like I wanted my life to end and so in this cabinet I often slept in, I attempted to hang myself. The most embarrassing and heartbreaking thing to me was that it was my young niece who found me and stopped me from taking my life. It was many incidents such as this that have truly shaped me into who I am today through the display of God's grace and His hand that covered me through it all. The saddest thing is that it would not be the last time I would be trapped into this mind game the devil played very well with me.

Attempts to Hide the Pain

There is no greater pain than the combination of wanting to be accepted and love - yet not knowing where you came from and not knowing why you cannot have all of these things. For many years growing up I had only known my mother, one aunt (I hardly ever saw), one sister and four brothers, along with nieces and nephews that would come along as time went by - but there was always something inside of me that just knew that "this cannot be it." This cannot be all that my family consists of. Although I wanted to find my other family members so badly, I decided to channel my energy into something that I thought was more productive. When I was in the seventh grade I began to join sports teams. By the time I was a senior in high school I had accomplished playing soccer, softball, cross country, track and field and the marching band. Anything I could do to keep busy and out of the house, I did it.

See growing up, my sister had her first child when I was about four years old and she lived with our mother for the longest. For years, I was raised side by side with many of my nieces and nephews, so naturally they were just there all the time. My brother had also had his fair share of children, but the only difference was he did not live with my mom. Well at least not too much at the time. By the time I was in high school I had a total of nine nieces and nephews. My mother had the biggest heart in the world, so she always took in her kids after they left and had kids of their own. Growing up I knew those who were around me all the time - but still had not known anyone else (including my father) existed out there, which was one of the biggest pieces missing from my heart.

There were so many people in our house that many times I just felt like I blended into the wall. I never thought anyone ever saw or paid attention to me. No one ever came to my band competitions, cross country or track and field meets. As much as I dearly love her, my own mother came late to my graduation. When I graduated from high school, I was a pretty rare young adult. I was a very hard working, selfless (yes I know this concept is rare, my employers out of high school thought the same thing!) Also a teen who was still a virgin!

Now today that is almost unheard of, as we know many young people have lost the value of self-respect and willingness to wait for anything. My first actual job I ever had was working at McDonalds. Since I was a child I have always mastered just about anything I put my hands to, so naturally with working at McDonalds I was a pro. Flipping burgers may not be a hot idea to many, but at that point in my life I was content with finally having my own money to control. One of the biggest life lessons was birthed while working at this job. Between the desire to be useful and the love of working, I worked more overtime than I can count. I was always willing to pick up the slack or shifts just as quickly as they were willing to offer (not to mention I had a crush on my boss Eric!).

One of the results (mind you I did NOT say blessings) of working the overnight shift, was meeting my first official boyfriend. We will call him JUJU #1. My former Pastor Chuck used 'juju' as a means to describe a no-good young man. My juju

#1 was very appealing to the eye. A very handsome-looking young fellow who was smooth to the core. He was checking me out as I served him and I was very flattered by his smooth talk. His uncle Skip - who accompanied the passenger side, seemed to really be interested in us hooking up, so he continued to push for the cause. So we exchanged numbers.

Now mind you I had never had a boyfriend before, so I had no idea what to do with this guy. It started off very sweet and innocent. We did not spend much time together during the day, but that did not faze me. We would spend countless hours during the day texting because he was "unable" to come and visit me until usually after 1 am. I was very sheltered growing up so none of these things really threw up red flags for me. I was truly young and dumb.

I did not see the need to be cautious until I received a call from the county jail. Yes that's right the Allegheny County Jail! Being the foolish and inexperienced young woman I was, I went and bailed him out of jail. I called myself being in love and was more than willing to do anything for him to show him I was his "ride or die chick".

That day I sat at the jail for hours waiting for him to be processed and the end result was not even a thank you, barely a hug and strange looks from his family who came as he was being released only to give him a ride home as I was on my way to work. I had not known the reason at this point for his incarceration. I just knew I "loved" him and would do whatever was needed to show it. Apparently bailing him out when his family refused to help was showing him who really cared, or so I thought. I thought that somehow after spending the hundreds I paid by myself with my McDonalds job to get him out, that I would really have some favor with him; that he would love and appreciate me more, that his family would root for him to keep me around. Little did I know things would soon change drastically and only for the worst.

Juju #1 was the one to whom I lost my virginity. See here is where I firmly believe that a father's love could have prevented this from taking place. At the time I had not realized how much he did not value me - and truthfully speaking, I had not really valued myself too much either.

That night was no special night by any means. He took me to a local motel (as we were jitneyed by his Uncle Skip and his right-hand man). It was a very cheap place off in the woods. You know one of those places you see in the movie where someone is chopped up and buried in the woods. There were no candles burning softly or rose petals scattered around the room. It was an ugly, dingy and cold motel room. More like something out of a bad romance novel.

That night not much happened, but it was enough to start me on a bad cycle of trying to fill a God-sized void with sex. My void was previously filled with the accomplishments I made while playing sports and now that I had been introduced to the feeling of sexual intercourse, I was intrigued. I never grew to have a passion for this God-given gift, but I did my fair share.

After this night I began to see how strange things really got in our relationship. We never had sex again, but I became more of a money magnet for him and for some odd reason (now that I look back) I just cannot figure out how or why I was willing to LITERALLY hand over my checks to him. It was as if he was my pimp without the disgrace of me having to sell out my body. I just worked every two weeks for him with permission to at least pay my cell phone bill, to stay connected to him! It was not until later that I had found out many vital key things concerning who he was. As I mentioned before, he never spent time with me during the day and it was not until after he was put in jail that I realized it was because he was a drug dealer! Big shocker right?!? It was as if everyone knew, but me!

Now I had accepted Jesus Christ into my life when I was 13 years old. My mother would wake us up on Sunday mornings and drag us on the bus to whatever church the Spirit lead her to. My mother told all of us that we would go to church until we were eighteen years of age, which was when we were permitted to make our own decisions (at least concerning whether or not we would continue our relationship with Christ), but until then we had to listen to whatever she said. After I turned eighteen I did continue to go to church, but there was a point in which my mother no longer went to church for reasons unknown to me. Although my mother raised us by herself - by the grace of God, she never let us see a single project or ghetto. This allowed us to never have the 'project or ghetto mentality' so much so, that I am often called a 'white girl trapped in a black girl's body' (although I see nothing wrong with pronouncing words properly. Hence the reason I love words so much!).

My mother tried her very best to make sure that we were ok at all cost concerning the things we saw and heard, so having a boyfriend that was a drug dealer was a bit new to me. Eventually I also found out he had a whole family down south and I am not talking about a family as in 'brothers, sisters, mom and dad'. No, I am talking a few children and his woman. Now this was all mind-boggling to me. Too many times, we sit and look at situations many times from the outside in. We begin to sit back and judge, thinking "Doesn't she know any better", "Why can't she be smart and walk away", "I know what I would do". But when you are the one stuck in the situation, it is much tougher to make a decision that appears to be common sense to others who do not have to make them.

Now with who I am today, I would certainly come to the assumption of, "What the heck is any woman thinking to be willing to stay with or support a drug dealer," but at the time I did not know any better. It hurt A LOT not to be 'daddy's little girl' or to have him validate me, so I knew no better when the jujus of this world tried to spit their ever-so-lame game to me. The thing that hurt the most was knowing that the one thing my mother did fail at, was not taking the time to validate me when my father was not there. Now by all means, my mother was a good mom and the best to be honest. There were many days that were very rough growing up with her and many times I felt so mad at her that I said things I did not mean then or now - but one thing that was always missing was validation and affirmation. I also do not blame her for this. With my own parenting, I have come to see that these things do not just come natural. They have to be role-modeled. I never got it then and now that I look back, I realize it was something I needed the most. Again, it is very hard to expect someone to give you something that they have never had or simply something they do not know how to do, even if it seems simple to us. So without getting this from anyone who truly loved me, when a juju came along and told me that he loved me - followed by what I needed to do to show him how much I loved him in return, I accepted the proposition every time. I started having sex when I was eighteen years old and continued only until I was nineteen.

For JuJu #1 it lasted about a year. It got so bad that at one point I found myself being desperate to continue a relationship with him.

It was not until later I learned he was still living with his mother and jobless. I was pretty upset to say the least, but in spite of what I had seen thus far during the journey to his room, I still decided to hang out with him. I could not tell you what I expected to get out of this evening at all. Up to this point, he was not the finest thing out, but he was nice so maybe I could compromise and settle. He did at least show me a lot of kindness and hospitality - but isn't that how everyone is when they are new to people and seeking what they want? Well one thing lead to another and as I was laying with him in sin, I began to think in my head 'OH CRAP, I am not going to walk away from this one'.

When he took me home that night he expressed his desire to be in a relationship with me because he was "so in love". All I could say was, "Dude you're not even that cute. I never want to see you again". I know you're probably thinking this girl is the worst, but I warned you. I tend to be blunt sometimes with my words. I felt trapped. I mean this guy could still contact me and try to pursue me. I was trying to break this thing off easy and hope and pray that I was not pregnant as I thought I was - but to my demise, some weeks later I started feeling weird so I took a total of three pregnancy tests and they all came back clear as day POSITIVE. I never felt like a greater failure in my entire life. It was bad enough that at this time I had not finished any college education as I had planned, but to make matters worse I was pregnant.

I was very scared to tell my mother. I just did not know how she was going to react. At this time, she already had eight grandchildren so it wasn't like it was a big deal to add another to the mix, but I so badly wanted to be the one she could be proud of. I never saw this as being a reality for my life at this point. I could never see myself telling her or my oldest brother, or my older brother who had always been my biggest fan.

Eventually the time came when I couldn't wait any longer and I remember the day I told my mom. I remember the day very clear. I had taken her out on the porch and as I tried to figure out a way to tell her this news, my oldest brother had pulled up to the house. I was scared out of my mind of the reaction he would have, so I quickly blurted out what I had to say before he could even get out of his car. I remember my mom simply telling me she would be there for me, but the topic would be addressed later. It took me a few months to find the courage - but I told the rest of my family starting with my baby brother Dave and older brother Greg, who did not seem as disappointed as I thought they would be. I remember my older brother making light of the situation and reminding me of all the accomplishments I had made up until this point, which is something he has always been good at throughout my life.

I also eventually told juju #2, whose response had been that we needed to be in a relationship for the sake of the child to come. We were going to be a family now so we needed to make things work.

Now I was already stuck with him for the rest of my life, so I was pretty sure I was not going to add insult to injury by actually being with him. This idea did not make him very happy, so for my entire pregnancy and years to come, I dealt with one of the meanest and most difficult men I had ever met.

During my pregnancy, he did not attend a single doctor's appointment, which I was torn about. A major part of me was very happy because I never wanted to be seen in public with him, but a very big part of me was depressed every time I went into an appointment by myself. I felt like I became a statistic, which was everything I tried to avoid.

Here I am a 19-year-old single mother. I felt so ashamed every time I saw a couple and how happy the woman appeared to be to have the support of the child's father with her. Seeing how happy that couple appeared when they were facing the reality of getting something that they wanted, but there was one appointment in particular I will never forget. I remember going in by myself as usual and around this time, I was about seven months pregnant. During the visit, they told me that they found something. Now my biggest fear in the entire world during this pregnancy was that I would give birth to twins. I was a twin myself and the idea of giving birth to two babies almost sent me into shock. I allowed the doctor to do what they do best. They told me that they needed to complete a blood test. I was completely confused as to what was going on, but I agreed to whatever they needed me to do. I heard nothing of the results until the next doctor's appointment came around.

A few doctors came into the room, which made me feel really uncomfortable. This had never happened before on a checkup. They first apologized for the news they had to tell me, but announced that I had contracted a STD. During the first few checkups you have during a pregnancy, they check for all these things and initially with basic tests I was cleared because the disease never came up.

Prior to this visit I was so thankful to God that the only result of my sin was the baby. Now as I was being told that I had contracted a disease, I felt like I was near death. At that moment, I was so numb to all that was going on that I gave no response. I could not at that time. I did not know how to feel. I did not know what to say. I did not know what to do.

It was not until I was out of the doctor's appointment and I had walked a little ways away from the building, that I crouched down in a ball and began to cry unstoppable tears of dread, sorry, disgust and fear. I just could not believe that my life had come to this. I was not out sleeping around with multiple men or doing crazy things. This was this one time with this one guy and this was the result. So many young people around me walked away from their many partners with as little as a memory or notch in their belt. It just blew my mind that things could really come down to this.

That night I spent the night with one of my son's Godmothers (he had a total of 6 God parents when he was born. I was new to the process of selecting God parents and felt bad, so I kept adding people to the list. To this day only one Godmother remains).

I shared what happened with her and just cried. I could not believe why or how this could happen to me. She encouraged me to call him and ask if he knew. I braved myself for this daunting task then went downstairs and called him. I asked him if he knew he had this and how could he do this to me. His response was "I hope you and the baby die." I could not believe it. I felt like slowly my world was unraveling into a big mess that I could not control.

My son's Godmother was very comforting. She never treated me as though I was a freak of nature or any of the things I thought towards myself. She was the biggest source of emotional stability that I had in that moment. One of my first thoughts that really overwhelmed me was, 'what would any of the other youth from my church think about me had they ever found out about this' and the second thought that crippled me for years was, 'what man will ever want to touch a woman who has not only a baby, but a sexually-transmitted disease as well?' It had taken me a long time before I could tell any of my family members because I was so embarrassed. I was the one no one thought these things would ever happen to and here I was stuck in a lifelong situation that was humiliating and emotionally crippling.

As a result of this new discovery to my health, I had to be given medication to take during the duration of my pregnancy to ensure the disease never spread to my unborn child. About one month prior to his due date, my labor was induced due to my son being so tiny and not appearing to be gaining much weight during the course of my pregnancy. My mother and youngest brother went with me when I went into labor. I decided to go natural with no pain meds because not only do I not care for needles - but I had also heard from friends that things went wrong when they had epidurals, so I opted to deal with the pain of natural childbirth.

After my son was born I dealt with a rollercoaster of emotions quite often. I was so overwhelmed with the concept that I had a child. I mean he was cute which, was a plus and he was a boy which was an answer from God, but those things could never outweigh the fact that I was a mother at the age of 20 and I was not married.

Shortly after my son was born I decided to tell his dad. He was not invited to witness the birth for his absence during my pregnancy. When his family came to see my son the reaction of the family was, "Well this cannot be our grandson. Our son did not father this baby". This was just one of many headaches I endured with dealing with this family. Eventually we went through the whole paternity process and what do you know, it was proven 99.9% that he was the father. I knew I did not have to attend an episode of Maury to reveal that. Even after the issue of paternity was resolved, there still was not a lot of care from him to be involved in his son's life actively or even consistently - and as a result, on many occasions and during many sleepless nights I would get so frustrated, frustrated beyond reason.

I did not think it was very fair that I was the one who had to wake up by myself in the middle of the night to change diapers and feed a baby that I had not created myself. I hated my life. I felt like a complete and total failure. As a result of the terrible feelings I had and really a lack of being able to see God in my life, there were many times when my son would cry at night and all I saw was his father. Here I was a brown-skinned woman with an almost white- looking baby (he was the same complexion as his dad due to his dad being bi-racial).

I would try my best to maintain my emotions and calm my frustrations, but many times I just could not control myself, so I would violently shake my baby. All I wanted him to do was be quiet, so I would shake him. Not enough to commit 'shaking baby syndrome', but just enough to make him stop fussing (as if this rationale made any sense at all). Now I know you are reading this and thinking 'this terrible person', but let's be real - I am not the only person who has been here, married or not. See I had fed him, changed him, tried to comfort him and it seemed like nothing I did would work so I figured shaking him would do something in my favor.

Now let me show you how the grace of God works. There would be many times that although she was not a light sleeper, my mother would come into my room and take him off me. I would do my best to politely ask her to get out of my room (while living in her house) and attempt to persuade her that everything was ok, but she always saw right through that. She would just put out her hands and ask for the baby. She would go back into her room to rock him to sleep. I believe and know without a doubt that this was nothing but the spirit, grace and mercy of God that would wake my mother and intercede on behalf of not only myself - but for the sake of my son's life as well. It was as if my mom would creep down the usually loud hallway very quietly to take my son and rock him to sleep slowly as only a grandmother can do, so that I could get some rest and save me from making one of the biggest and uncorrectable decisions in my life.

Now I have to admit and I wish this was not true - but sadly, this happened on many occasions. I came to a place where I had so much frustration and anger in my heart. I had come to a place of allowing my heart to be hardened. I was emotionless and cold to everyone around me, including my son.

Over the course of his first five years of life, I went through constant battles of dealing with disrespect from my son's dad and grandmother, child support issues and the worst were the custody issues. I am one of those strong black women who you cannot just allow anything to happen without dishing something back in return. The hard part of that is the fact that I am and have been a woman of God since the age of thirteen, so I must be careful concerning the way I carry myself - but this never phased me during the early years of my son's life and my experience as a single mother.

Again, the disrespect started when I declined the opportunity to be in a relationship with my son's father when I found out I was pregnant. After I had my son, it progressed to times where he would talk disrespectfully to me and I would keep my son from him for periods of time. Now I know that young women and older women who are flat out immature tend to do this. We think we are doing something by keeping our child (ren) from their dads, as if this is a punishment to a man that is not taking care of his child willingly.

This is one of the many mistakes we make as women who have been scorned by a man and especially if there is a child involved. Let us be honest, we tend to use our children as bait and that is exactly what I did for the first couple of years of his life. At first, I would keep my son from his father just because I could not stand his father and used the power that I had against him. It later turned more into a safety issue for my son.

There were many times I would allow my son to go to his father's house and when his father got my son into his physical custody, he would refuse to allow me to have my son back. It became a regular thing between us. I would go to pick up my son, he or his mother would refuse to allow me to have my son and I would call the police. The most frustrating thing was that the police could never help. It was a matter that was out of their jurisdiction and they could only refer us to family court.

At one point they got so used to seeing me, they would tell me the same thing every time that they came out. There was nothing that they could do for me so I would either plead with him and his mother - call my mom screaming like a mad woman, or go home in tears frustrated because I felt like my hands were tied behind my back. It happened one too many times and when I would get him back, I eventually got to the point where I would just not allow my son to go over there - not just for reasons of custody, but because his father was not a very good influence for him.

His dad involved himself in unsafe activities that I did not want my son to see and has absolutely no respect for women, or his mother for that matter. See women, this is something we MUST pay attention to when we find a man who has become a point of interest to us. If he disrespects his mother and his mother does not do anything about it, there is no reason in the world that he would give more respect to some random female that he is not guaranteed to be with for the rest of his life and even a lifelong commitment may not truly be kept. The hardest part of being involved with this young man was that I was stuck with him. There was no opportunity to mess around and then never see him again. I was trapped and I hated it!

Now onto juju #3, who was by far the most secretive and misleading person I had ever met in my entire life. He literally led two lives and was one of those men that if it had not been for the grace of God, would have landed me on the show 'Snapped'! I met him off the same website as well (as you can see he was one of my many). I looked on his profile page one day and loved what I saw. I solely sought after him because of a few professional pictures he had, because man he looked good. I mean he looked so good that I thought he was a model and I knew in my mind that I would NEVER be able to get with a guy of his caliber, but I thought I could at least try.

See this is what the enemy will do to you if you are not careful. He will show something that only appears to look appealing (after it has been 'doctored up' of course) just to suck you in. He looked fine as wine (one of my favorite quotes!) or so I thought. I contacted him on the website through a private message and we started talking back in 2008, just shortly after I had my son.

We made it through the honeymoon stage that all relationships go through. Things seemed to be going very well. He was a nice guy, a few years older than me (which is what I like in a man) and had a college education, which as we all know is a major plus. By far the best thing I had met at that point of my life, but over the time period of 2008 to 2013 things had changed.

After I got comfortable with him, I felt compelled to tell him news that would be certain to change the way things were in the relationship and most likely for the worst. When I finally came to a place to be able to tell him I had contracted a sexually-transmitted disease, his reaction was not nearly as bad as I thought it would be. He seemed very understanding, informing me that everything would be ok. He insisted that if he came to the table with a child, he would work with me through this hard time in his life. I had later come to realize that he was willing to accept that I was not going to have sex with him until marriage - because he was having sex with another young woman, making it acceptable for him to not get this fulfillment from me.

We would talk off and on, more off than on. We argued as if we were a married couple many times for the most stupid reasons. Many of the arguments stemmed from the fact that he just never came to see or spend time with me. See we lived in two different counties and at this point I had never been invited to meet his family or friends.

He had always complained that it was too far for him to drive out here to me and that he had too much to do and my foolish self always listened. This excuse was only temporary. We argued about the lack of his presence in my life from time to time, but for the most part I just accepted that what he was telling me was the honest truth. He was also the type (well at least he said he was) that wanted to make sure he took care of all that was his - and what woman would not be attracted to a man who appears to truly be a man?

Early on in the relationship I learned that he had a daughter, which was not a huge deal to me seeing as though I had a son. He also had the issue of having a hard time finding employment in the field he studied in college. Seeing as though he could not find a job in the Pittsburgh area, he decided he would move out of the state. At this time, I did not want to seem selfish but I did not really care for or like the idea, but understood he needed to do what was best for himself and his daughter. By all means, we were not married and she came first.

One major incident we had was when he announced a few days before he was leaving, that he would be traveling to the Washington, DC area to find a job. Now I was not very happy about this. I mean I knew things had not been the best between us, but the least I thought I deserved was a decent heads up that he would be up and moving to another state. It was not like it was another county. It was another state, but none the less he would not be here. I thought I had issues before of not being able to see him living in another county, but it would not compare to the issues we would have with him being so far away.

While he was out of state, I had spoken to him one night at work. I remember him telling me about his travels and all that he was trying to accomplish and I was very happy for him. His success meant a lot to me, but during this conversation, he asked me something that I had always desired, but never thought would happen over the phone. If I am being honest, he never asked it over the phone or in person. He had later TEXTED and asked me to marry him. Now this was and still is, one of the biggest desires of my heart.

Now yes he asked me to marry him actually through a text, but at the time I was the happiest girl in the world. I just could not believe what appeared to be the man of my dreams, was actually thinking of spending the rest of his life with little old me - but shortly after, reality began to set in. He wanted me to pick up everything and leave where I was and all that I had accomplished in my life to be with him.

The thought of this was fun and exciting briefly, but then I had to snap back to reality. I had a son for whom I was the sole provider and caretaker. The thought of uprooting him from all we knew was a big no for me, especially due to the fact that he was state-hopping because of his financial instability. I just knew saying yes to him would set me up for failure in the end. I had a job where I was. It was not the greatest job, but it was my full-time job with benefits and I actually liked the work I did.

I could not imagine walking away from this all. One of the things that really weighed heavy on my heart - and truly still does to this day, was that I was not certain with everything in my mind, body and soul that he was the one. I mean he looked real good and I knew I would look good with him, but I was afraid of divorce.

I made the decision to decline his text proposal. Although I had declined the opportunity to marry him at that time, I just knew that if he got himself stable things would improve and we would truly have a chance.

Over the next couple of years all we did was fight, argue and make up and then fight again. I would get so fed up with him that at times we would not speak to one another for months at a time and then due to my lack of self-control or willingness to see my value, I would find him through whatever means available such as old texts or good old Facebook and try to ignite a flame that had way past died.

Now as you know by now when I was growing up I did not have my father, but I had two exceptional men in my life who had become my spiritual fathers who have greatly contributed to who I am today (of whom I will go into greater detail in the next section). These two men loved me as if I were their own and showed me the love of God that is forever outgoing, faithful and consistent. One of them was a former pastor of mine. I had been with his ministry for eight years of my saved life. He was truly a man after God's own heart. He had a heart of gold, a smile that could bring you out of any funk and a hug that would take your breath away (literally).

During the course of our dealings this young man became upset many times because of the fact I was connected to my Pastor Chuck's son, who had dated his ex at some point in his life (just confusing stuff that I did not want to deal with). Now what this really had to do with me is unknown, but it surely did not sit well with me. I loved my pastor and his son very much and the thought that I would have to choose between the two, was ridiculous and very overwhelming. He took it so far as to say that we could not be married by my pastor because he would not allow his ex-girlfriend's ex-boyfriend's father to marry us. I know, too much drama right? Say that fast five times!

When he said this to me, I became enraged. How dare he tell me that my pastor and spiritual father could not marry us? I just knew Pastor Chuck would be the one to marry me when the time came. I did not care who the man was going to be, but if he was not willing to allow my Pastor Chuck to marry us - then clearly he was not the one. So I came to the conclusion he just was not the one for me. This was one of many times that we had not spoken to each other for months - but yet again, something inside me would tell me that we needed to reconnect, so once again we reconnected.

One looking from the outside in would think, 'What is wrong with this chick?'-but you see, it is much easier to look from the outside in on someone's situation and tell them what needs to happen next versus being the one to face the situation head on.

So as usual, we started speaking again and little do you know we would soon not be speaking AGAIN, but this time in particular was different. It was the beginning of 2010. I was participating in the fast the church conducted at the beginning of the year. This is a very common thing for most churches. This helps us to corporately get in sync with the will and plan of God for our lives that year.

Night services were very common for us, especially during a time of revival or fasting and prayer. During one of the night services; I heard a word that rocked me to the core. I remember the speaker addressing those individuals who set people as their "back-burner option". These were people who dealt with someone only in the event they had not found someone better.

In my heart of hearts I always felt as though juju #3 was doing this to me, but I never wanted to believe that after all this time it was really true. I was too good to him. I had finally come to a place of having at least a little bit of self-respect for myself after all I had gone through previously with my father, my son's dad and many failed previous relationships. I did not and could not believe this could be happening to me. I just knew he was the one, but at this point there was a little more in me that said I deserved better and was not willing to settle for less.

After that service, I spoke with a friend because my heart was heavy as I faced the reality that I was most likely his 'back-burner option' and needed to let go. She told me I needed to let him go, which seemed like the end of the world for me. I was still fighting this as I gave every excuse in the book and tried to justify him.

While growing up I was very different from most, if not all the people I was around - including my family. I did not date a lot in the sense of having a committed relationship where both parties acknowledged a commitment. Meeting juju #3 and having the opportunity to have anyone pay attention to me, I took it. In spite of his lack of commitment to me, I did not want to let go what we had (or so what I thought we had), no matter how hard those words spoken hit me.

Music is the biggest source of release in my life. There is a song for everything and mood. So when I went home that night I listened to the music I knew would make me cry, as I prepared to separate myself from the one I knew who was only keeping me as his 'back- burner option'.

Later that evening I had mustered up enough courage to return his missed call. While speaking to him, he immediately picked up that something was wrong. As I began to share with him all that I had learned and received from the service, I explained to him that I felt as though I was his 'back-burner option' and that I deserved better from him or any man and maybe it would be best for us to part ways. His response was "Well if your pastor has a better word for your life than I do, marry him."

This tore me to pieces. I could not believe the words that were coming out of his mouth, but at this time it was a clear indication of where he was mentally and spiritually. Later I told my Pastor Chuck what was said because it truly tore me up. I always went to Pastor Chuck for counsel. He encouraged me that this young man was not the one and God had simply showed me what I needed to see at this time concerning this situation. Here I am around the age of 20 years old, a single mother and cannot seem to find a decent guy to save my life. It depressed me more than anything that he was not the one I wanted him to be.

Sadly, this episode only stopped me from talking to juju #3 for about ten months before we started speaking yet again. While I was in this situation for all these years, I know I was torturing myself but it had not occurred to me that I needed to be smarter with the decisions I was making. In my own mind, I was making the best decisions I could make concerning dealing with this young man, but now I can see how wrong I really was.

An important thing I have learned over the years is that the bible clearly tells us, *"But seek first the kingdom of God and His righteousness, and all these things will be added to you."* Matthew 6:33 ESV. This scripture has been very helpful for me over the years. See when I look at this scripture, it reminds me of the simple concept that we MUST, MUST, MUST seek God in every single thing that we do. We must seek Him over the desires of our hearts. We cannot choose to not seek God, then get upset AT GOD when things do not work out the way we fantasize or conjure up in our minds.

Up to this point in my life, I had not sought God or His will in many - if not any of the situations that I had come across in my life. I always jumped into situations because I thought it would work out in my favor, because it was something I wanted or wanted God to want for me. It was not until after this situation that I realized I could have saved myself years of hurt and pain, had I simply sought God who already knew my end before my beginning.

As if I had not already been through enough drama in this situation - for whatever reason, in the beginning of 2012 I started speaking to juju #3 yet again, had I only known this would truly be the last time I would put myself in this situation (or so I thought!). This time it was truly different, at least in the beginning.

I had met him back in 2008. Over the course of the four years I had known him, I had never met his daughter, his family or had ever gone out with him anywhere. Well let me take that back. I have to give him a little bit of credit. When I first met him initially, he had taken me out to eat at a Chinese restaurant in the Downtown Pittsburgh area. So he did a little something, but this would be the only time he had ever taken me out.

At some point things had not worked out as he planned when traveling out of state to find work, so he returned home. Four years after our very first date, he finally invited me to come to his church, where his father was the pastor. Now at this time I thought I would be struck down if I had ever missed a day of church at the ministry I attended. I had never before missed a Sunday service to be anywhere else, but I was madly in love with this character and jumped at the opportunity to hang with him. I traveled all the way to his church and when I say traveled, I mean this was an hour drive that I took to see him and to be quite honest - I was instantly able to appreciate why he hardly ever came to see me. I mean I know he was not living in another state, but goodness he lived far away and gas is not cheap!

This particular weekend his family had a family reunion. At the end of that service I was going to leave, but his family had encouraged me to come back to their house. When I got there, I met his whole family; his aunts, uncles, cousins, parents and even his daughter. I was completely amazed. I felt like I was on cloud nine. I thought this would be it. I was in there like swimwear. His family appeared to be accepting me and I was pretty excited to be accepted and finally getting what I wanted.

For the next couple of months things went very well. I mean surprisingly well. We were communicating very effectively and for the first time in four years, he finally admitted that he was willing to commit and try to make things work. I was more than happy.

That Sunday I went home with a smile from ear to ear. I was so happy that I would FINALLY be getting what I had wanted from him for so long. Little had I known that in a short few months, things would change for the worse.

Around June of that year he went on vacation with his family. I remember this like it happened yesterday. I went onto good old Facebook and for some reason, I felt so compelled to check out his profile. There was one post I saw on his profile that confused me to no end.

One day while on vacation with his family, he wrote "Thank God my little man is finally here." Now this confused me because he had admitted he wanted to try to make things work with me and I had not had sex with any male in four years - so where the heck did this baby come from? I wanted to know what son was he speaking of. Sometimes I like to play dumb, so as I played stupid I texted him saying "Congrats on your little man" and he simply responded "Thank you." Now I was really confused at his response, so I dug a little deeper. I mean he made it seem as though I had known and been ok with what was going on. Now his older brother had a few children of his own, so I was thinking - was this his little man or a family member's new baby?

After he was prompted he started to explain that it was his baby, but he could not tell me previously because he did not want to mess up what we had so far. We were finally at a place where we were getting along, civil and could really make things work. I mean it was cute that he wanted to protect what we had, but what confused me is that if he did not tell me then - exactly when would he tell me about a whole other life he had created?

When he came back from vacation, he had slowed his communication down to almost nothing. After some time, I went back to his church without a heads up. At this point I felt comfortable enough with his family and figured a face to face confrontation would force him to give me answers that I wanted.

Another moment that I remember was one Sunday while visiting him it was raining very heavy. After the service he walked me to my car. This time I was not invited to his home. Due to the rain, we sat under a covering on the side of his church. At this time I had become comfortable enough in my own skin to be able to accept rejection and I told him, "If you do not want to be with me just tell me." and of course his response was that he wanted to make things work and that he just needed some time to get himself together.

Prior to me attending church with him and his family this Sunday, someone I went to church with told me they had a dream of a wedding and I was the bride. They told me different parts of the dream that they could remember. They never saw the groom's face, but there were faces from the crowd she saw. She kept speaking of a woman in a purple outfit with a big purple hat to match.

For some reason, I mentioned the mother of juju #3 and I showed her a picture that had him and his parents in it. She seemed to instantly recognize his mother from the dream although she had never met this woman before. Hearing these parts of the dream and knowing things were going so well, I made this dream to fit him and the desires I had. I did not have anyone else in my life that even came close to marriage material (as if he was), so I just assumed he was it.

A few months later - although we were barely speaking, I had gotten busy with an outreach that we had been doing at our church yearly. It was a fun and 'out of the box' kind of way to save souls and all who were involved with it loved it. It was what we waited all year to do.

During this time, all we did was this event. We did not really have time to date (unless you were already in a relationship); we did not have time to go to the movies and hang out on weekends or barely even sleep. All we did was this ministry event. Because I was doing this ministry, I hardly had time to travel to see him. During the month that we did this event, I did not want to fellowship with any other church other than my own in fear that I would miss something, so I had not seen him until about mid-November.

When I finally visited his church - I did not warn him ahead of time, I just went. When I got there, I felt very much out of place. It was very different. His mother had not been as warm and welcoming as she normally was when she saw me; his dad, brothers and cousins did not speak, but even he did something I never saw coming. As I walked into the church, he looked back. It was a very small church in which you knew everything that happened, including every time the front door opened and closed.

When I saw him, I got happy and a smile came over my face. I truly loved this person with all of my heart, but quickly I could see that he did not feel the same way. When he saw me, he never got up to hug me or greet me. He simply turned his head back to the front of the church to see who had entered and turned back around. I was appalled. I could not believe what was happening to me. I felt like I was the star of that show "Punk'd". I am not one for making a scene, so I found a seat a couple pews back from him and sat down with my son.

Now what really confused me was the fact that he was sitting next to a young female. Now can I be really, really honest with you? This had been the center of many of our arguments throughout the years. I knew that he was into dating outside of our race. Now by all means I am not racist at all - but for the life of me, I could not see what he saw in me if he had never dated a black female before me. Being who I am, I like to watch things so I sat back and watched how they interacted with one another.

He did not appear to be the happiest around her, but from the pictures I had seen on his Facebook, I gathered that she was the mother of his newest child. I kind of just told myself it is what it is and that I needed to do everything I could to enjoy the service while I was there. It was funny because his dad happened to be speaking about people being honest and keeping their word as God has done and will continue to do. Wasn't that a slap in the face for him to get that particular word on that particular day?

After the service, he still had not spoken to me. I tried to get out of the church as fast as I could, but it seemed like all of his family wanted to check and see how I was doing, but him. So I used the excuse that my son was being out of control (although many times it is just how he acts) so I could finally leave, have a chance to think things through and figure out why things had gone the way they did. I went home that day and I felt very heavy about what had happened.

I was in the process of sending him a Facebook message when something told me to read his profile. When I read it, I felt my heart pass through my stomach and hit the floor as it shattered into pieces. I read his relationship status which had changed some time prior from single to ENGAGED.

I could not even believe what I was reading. I read through some of the posts on his profile to see the communication between the two. See this is one of the many evils of Facebook in my opinion. While reading through his profile and knowing the first-hand experiences I had with him, I quickly realized that to him, I just never existed. This enraged me - I just could not believe that this was happening to me of all people. I had wasted so many years of my life for nothing.

Sleeping around with a lot of different men was not really my thing and I hardly ever dated. In spite of the hurt and frustration I felt all the way down to my soul, I mustered up enough courage and the words to say to him. Words and things I had wanted to express over the past 4 years. The most painful blow was seeing that he claimed to have been in a relationship with this female since 2008, which was the same time that we had been speaking off and on.

After some tears and a lot of screaming, I finally found the strength to send him a private message on Facebook (which was the only communication I had with him at this point. I deleted his number more times than I can count) telling him how hurt, frustrated and mad I was because of all that I had endured from him. His response was that I was being overly dramatic and that he never meant to hurt me. This was the second most hurtful thing I had ever dealt with in my whole entire life. I could not believe that someone I gave my heart to for the past four years would treat me as though I was no better than the gum under his shoes.

The Church: 'Imperfect people serving a perfect God'

I received salvation when I was thirteen years old. Depending on the person, their parents (or lack thereof), their home life and many other contributing factors - a person can come to the realization of the need for salvation at any time in their life. No matter how young or old the person is, when this happens it is always an amazing thing to experience.

For me, receiving salvation was one of those things that at the time I did just because my mom had done it at some point in her life and I trusted what she did. I remember my first pastor and his wife (which would be the first of many spiritual leaders over the course of my saved life). They were the nicest people I had ever met, but the only thing I had not liked about this church was that it was full of old people. Now I have not a single problem with the elderly, but to be quite honest - not having many young people to connect with when you are young and saved does not really help one to grow.

It was while under this ministry that I developed a general and very basic foundation of who God was and received water baptism. During this time in my life, I had come to the conclusion that it was a good idea to be saved, but had not truly understood the importance of it all and how it would truly affect my life when I decided to give God my all. Therefore over the next three years, I would spend a lot of time waking up early Sunday morning to get on the bus and travel to wherever the Lord led my mother that day along with my siblings, niece and nephew.

Many times it was so irritating because there were about seven of us total, which meant seven times the hassle. There was everyone getting dressed in the morning; getting something to eat, then we all walked to the bus stop, climbed on the bus, found seats, watched my mom pour all the money into the money machine, got off the bus taking forever and a year and then straggled into whatever church my mom found for us to go to at that time - which at times I was a fan of and many times I was not.

Among all the churches my mom had taken us to, there is one in particular I will never forget. It was at this church, I met the man who would become my first father figure (whom I will call Super Dad!) I had ever known in my life. He had a wife and two boys. One was my age and the other was a little bit older than us, so I never really saw him or got to know him too well due to him being away at college out of state.

I was about sixteen years old when I met this family. I was very shy and did not have very much confidence or self-esteem, so I never really held my head up when I spoke to people. I never dressed outrageously nice due to the single income from my mother and multiple bodies that needed to be clothed. My family did not have a lot of money or status so it was not like we were all that big of a deal - but little did I know that with this family my world, as I knew it, would change in so many ways.

None of my siblings ever really caught interest into the saved life like I had. At this point in our lives our mother mandated that we go to church at the very least until we were 18 years of age. For me this was not that big of a deal. Now looking back I can see that it was certainly one of many ways I used to escape my home life, so I did not mind being at the church or around church folks all the time. In a short period of time I became very close to this family. I cannot tell how or why we came to this place - but I became so close, that shortly after my mom and all of my other family members who were going to church had stopped attending church and I never stopped to care or ask why.

I was caught up in my own moment and my own world. I had finally had a father figure I could call my own. I mean he was not my own biological father, but this experience was close enough and I absolutely loved it. Granted he had two children of his own and a wife, but Super Dad called me his daughter, treated me as such and I loved it more than words could ever express. His family was very open and loving to me. His sons treated me just like their sister. We argued like brother and sister and we supported one another at school events like brother and sister. All the things I had not been able to experience with my brothers, I was able to do with them.

Super dad helped me with homework, took me to church, hung out with me and allowed me to eat Sunday dinners with his family. To some this may not seem like a big deal, but to me I felt like I was on cloud nine. I was finally "like" the other kids. I was on top of the world. It was through this man that I had my hair done professionally for the first time. Again to some it is not much of a big deal, but for me it made me feel so beautiful. I remember hating the process (as I do now), but once I was done I had come to find a sense of confidence. I could finally be happy with who I was. I could look in the mirror or take pictures and smile without it being forced.

I never had the opportunity to be taught how to do my own hair, so many times I looked as though no one at home really loved me. Again I know my mother did, but I also know that there have been many times when I have looked at kids that did not look as well kept and thought, 'that parent must not care a lot about their child'. Due to not knowing how and clearly not having that gift, I never really tried to do anything for myself (outside of frying my hair with hot combs and perms) and I never had the money to get my hair done. All in all this was the start of my confidence being built and I appreciated that more than my Super Dad probably realizes.

Over the next few years, I would begin to spend more time with this family than I did with my natural family. I do not know if my mother was ever upset about it, but I knew my mom trusted this family. Ultimately she never said anything about the time I was spending with them, which made me very content because like many young ladies I was very nice and easy to please - but I could also be a brat and quick to throw a fit when I did not get what I wanted.

Their sons truly became my brothers. It was like I was living two different lives. In one of those lives, I was the youngest girl that no one gave too much attention to or even covered as being the youngest. I had nappy hair and cheap clothes that were very few in number. In my other life I felt like I was daddy's little girl. I had someone in my life that was not looking to hurt me. He simply wanted to build up the self-esteem I never had, bring me to a place of self-respect and allow me to grow in my relationship with God.

At times I felt torn between the two worlds - but in spite of that I still felt secure that no matter what happened, I was loved and would never be hurt. I was secure that no matter what happened I still had someone who cared for me no matter where I was.

As I was accustomed to, I went to church at Down the Street Gospel Center with them every Sunday for a few years until they decided they were going to move on from the church where we had been for about a year or so. At Down the Street Gospel Center, they did something very cool called tent revivals. They would set up a huge tent a little distance from the church in a parking lot and have church services under this tent. Down the street Gospel Center also had an older feel or spirit to it.

Many churches do church in different ways. Some have revivals, some skits, some dance, some sing and some act. At this church we had tent revivals and one evening in particular, I saw something that at this point I had never seen before while saved. A couple of young men that came to minister at the revival were on fire for God and I knew that when I saw them I just wanted what they had. I wanted to be where they were. I mean to me this energy that they had for God was astonishing. I had been to churches whose members were much older than I was and many times in these churches, they tend not to have as much energy for God as a church that had more youth in its attendance. Again, there is NOTHING wrong with those who are older, but as a young person I desired to be entertained (which is not what God has called us to be).

To keep a young person saved, it is very vital to have a bit of a youthful ministry to hold their interest. Not to conform to the ways of young people or the world - but to be willing to do whatever it takes (as long as it's pleasing to God) to hold their attention and attendance, or the world will do a pretty decent job for us.

Although I had been jolted with this inspiration of radical youthfulness for Christ, I continued to stay with the current ministry until my spiritual father announced that we would be leaving to find another ministry. I did not understand what was going on at the time, but I trusted them and went along with whatever they said.

During these Sunday mornings, my dad would pick me up and then we would travel back to his house to get the rest of the family and head to whatever church God lead them to. It seemed like it was déjà vu all over again, but this time it was not as bad. This time I was sitting in the back seat of the car with my brother hoping and praying that we would go to the ministry where the young men were from, only to be disappointed Sunday after Sunday.

Finally, one Sunday my biggest heart's desire had come to pass. I remember putting my head down as my dad drove. I was dreading where we would visit next and I just knew we were going to a church that I most likely would not enjoy. I was not sure where we were headed, but I knew we would end up at some foreign ministry where I would be subject to being an outsider yet again. This particular Sunday when the car came to its final stop, I could not believe my eyes. It was like Christmas early or maybe that excitement you get when you get something you never thought you would ever get.

We pulled up to the church I had longed to visit and I was so ecstatic. I tried to hide my extreme excitement but when we went in, I just loved the atmosphere. Now I was very nervous to be in a new place, but it was very youthful and spontaneous. Although I had been connected with my spiritual father for years now, I just knew I wanted and needed to be connected to this church.

At this point in my life I made one of the very first grownup decisions for myself. I made the decision that I would be staying at this ministry. I am not sure how everything came to be - but before I knew it, I was joining as a member of this ministry and totally loving my new life.

To tell you the truth, some 8 years later I honestly cannot even begin to tell you how I came to the decision that I made. At that time in my walk with God, I was not mature enough to know that I needed to pray to God before making a decision in my life and not just for the things we consider being major. I mean taking EVERYTHING to God in prayer.

Most things that we are involved with during the course of our lives tend to start out awesome in bit of a honeymoon period - but many times can end as a train wreck where no one really knows what, why, how or when things went wrong.

During the early years in the ministry I did not do much - but as I became more seasoned and more familiar with the other members, leadership and youth, I did it all. I was in the fine arts department, which included dancing, skits and dinner theaters. At one point I had convinced leadership of my ability to properly clean and care for the church. I assisted the pastor's aide committee from time to time. When we grew beyond capacity for the building they purchased and began to rent out a space, I took on the job of setting up and breaking down the church every Sunday. I was a greeter, a Sunday school teacher and did just about anything I could do to help the ministry.

One thing I love about being me is that I am a busy person who loves to be involved and being useful - so whatever I could do to help, I was there many times before they could voice the need for help. I mean I was so eager to help, that at one point in my life I came to live very close to the church. So close that many times I would peek out my window to see if anyone was at the church. If I saw someone's car I would race to put on my shoes, get my son together (if he was with me) and head on over to see what I could do to help. I mean it was to the point where I ended up having keys due to the duties I had with the church. During certain functions I would go HOURS early or stay late to setup, break down and attempt to take as much stress as possible off others, especially those in leadership.

I made the decision to live so close to this ministry because it was easier for me and prevented me from having to ask for a ride to church from someone who did not want to and was mostly likely not willing to; it also prevented me from having to catch multiple buses with a child. Not to mention the landlord that I had was more than awesome. There were many times I could not pay my rent that month or pay it on time and he always told me not to stress about it, to make sure my son and I were ok. Not to mention, the year he lowered my rent without reason to help me financially.

The major problem with the first 4 years of my attendance with this ministry was that, although I did all I thought I was supposed to do concerning church protocol and being involved - it was not until years later that I realized I never did what Christ requires from us when He tells us that our hearts and minds must be renewed.

Although I was in a church full of young people, somehow I still found myself as an introverted outsider. I did anything to get attention and fit in. At this point, I was also living a double life. In church I was a very shy, yet outgoing helpful young person - but at home as stated previously, I went on multiple websites to find what I thought was love. When we focus too heavily on what we can do for others in the church, without giving any focus on how Christ wants to deal with us as individuals, we become very lost IN the church without knowing it. We tend to do many things, thinking that these things will somehow buy acceptance, grace, mercy, merit or favor; when in reality, we are digging ourselves into a self-made pit of what may later become bitterness and regret that can possibly uproot any firm foundation we thought we had in this walk.

Due to not being able to truly fit in at church among the youth and not being close to any of my family members, or really having any true friends to call my own - I found someone who would pay attention to me, which then led to the pregnancy with my son.

See when I mention being able to fit in, one thing that always bothered me as I mentioned before, is 'cliques' that we have in churches. For whatever reason, we tend to not always look at one another as brothers and sisters in Christ worthy of the fellowship we so desperately need in this walk. Befriending one another is almost like picking out the latest trends in clothing. We go and look at what looks to be the most suitable, hip, or fashionable - not taking into account or consideration what it is made of or what fruit it could bear in our lives. So many times what we think looks good, we take (although many times the fruit that is produced is funky) and what appears to be not as appealing is left behind - when in reality it can end up being the most flattering piece of clothing we could have ever tried on had we given it a try.

Although I had not been given the opportunity to have many close friends, at this church I did find myself becoming close with two people - who although were good friends, had two separate and shocking reactions to being new additions in my life. I struggled with telling anyone about the life-changing decision I had made. I did not want people to judge me, walk out on me, or turn their backs on me and I knew for sure that abortion was not an option.

I did not know what to do, but knew I had this thing bottled up inside of me begging to get out. I felt heavy every time I talked to someone because I knew the state of deception that I lived in. When I was at church I appeared to be a very sweet and innocent church girl, but outside the church I was a young woman driven by a desperate and lonely pursuit of flesh that I did not know how to control.

The day I finally mustered up enough courage to share the news with the first person, I received a reaction I never thought I would get. It hurt more than words could say. Slinky and I had become pretty close, sharing similar experiences, thoughts and feelings. I really thought I was going to receive more support, but I ended up feeling as though I was the biggest freak of nature and sinner out of the youth and I felt like I was the only one who sinned in that church. (It is funny how many times those doing the most dirt will make light of others and their dirt, in order to take light or attention off themselves for the sake of buying more time to live it up in sin).

I was tremendously embarrassed. I felt worse after I told slinky than I did when I tried to keep it to myself. I wanted to crawl into a small space and just die. I remember looking into his eyes when I finally shared the news. His face changed immediately and for the rest of the day his demeanor towards me was so different. I did not know what to do with myself. I just knew that any hope of fitting in or having a true friend in this difficult time had been obliterated.

The next person I told was much more comforting and encouraging. Little treated me as though I was a person who simply made a bad decision and encouraged me that I could and would recover from it. Little was one of very few that I could actually call a friend and know that he would never do anything to hurt me.

When I shared the news with Little, he told me that he would always be there for me and my child no matter what. Over the first couple of years of my son's life, Little was not around a lot - but when he was, it was as if he had been around the entire time. He was so loving and fun to be around, that it did not matter how much time passed when he was not around us. When we reconnected it was like we never missed a beat of one another's lives.

In 2006 when Little died, it was one of the hardest things to hit me. I was at work on the 3-11 shift when I found out. A church member had posted "RIP Little" on their profile. I was confused, because you know sometimes people know more than one person with the same name. I prayed that this was a person I had not known. As I frantically tried to get an answer, I finally got the dreadful confirmation that it was Little. I cried my entire shift. I was so devastated. The one true friend who did not judge me or ever mistreat my son was gone. This created a hole in my heart.

One of the hardest things about being a part of this ministry, was that I did not have any real connections to anyone or the ministry itself. I came from nowhere, did not have any money, I was not related to anyone from the ministry, did not grow up with anyone or date anyone. I was just an outsider who got pregnant.

Now let's indulge in a moment of complete and total honesty. Here is something that many churches do not want to acknowledge or admit: CHURCHES HAVE TOO MANY CLIQUES. Oh my goodness... No she didn't... Yes I did. This is the truth whether or not people want to admit it. There are the pastor's kids and those close to them, there are the pretty girls, musicians or jocks and so many other cliques depending on the denomination of the church.

Yes, I know it sounds a lot like high school all over again right? Only in the church, it is a spiritual high school with a bunch of people giving the impression that they are much better off spiritually than most - even when they claim to have humility. It happens no matter how big or small the ministry is and this is the reality that I faced during the early years of my saved life.

I felt like I could not escape a clique. Whether it was in church or in school, they very much existed. Oddly enough, it was easier to be connected to a clique in school than it was to be connected to those who were saved! Crazy right?

With that being said, not only was I already an outsider by default, I became even more estranged from the rest of the youth in our ministry due to me now having an addition to my life that would be noisy, time and money-consuming. It stopped me from being able to sit in a service and get the word because of a screaming and fussy baby and later toddler, who just chose to 'show his butt'. It stopped me from being able to hang out as much as I wanted to because of many who had a sense of discomfort with being around a young adult who had a child. I mean it truly is no fun when you're having the time of your life and you have to stop to feed, burp or change a diaper. It is sad to say, but I was the first one out of our youth group to start the not-so-cool trend of being a "baby's mama" and trust, this was NOTHING to be proud of.

Perfectly Imperfect | 58

Over the years, I would attempt to juggle many issues that most of the youth I had been in church with had not even come close to dealing with. I was going in and out of court for child support, battling mentally and emotionally-brutal issues of custody, battling the stability of being able to provide food, having a low income and keeping a roof over our heads.

It hurt many times to see how people would treat me and my son. Many put up with us because they had to, but the reaction of some were so hurtful that I did all I could to laugh it off defenselessly in public - but I would be brought to my knees in tears in private. They treated my situation as though many of them were not having sex themselves and could have faced the same results of their decisions as I had. There were many I knew that had enough sex to produce at least three or four kids and receive sexually transmitted diseases from all the people they had slept with.

One of the things I regret the most about my previous experiences in the church world, is that I never had a covering. After leaving the covering of my spiritual father, I had no one to stick up for me or care that I was being mistreated in ways I know hurt God. There were many times I was belittled, judged, talked about to my face and behind my back (some coming from those in positions of authority in the church). I was left out, used and abused. When I joined this ministry I joined by myself, then later had a kid - so I was not the most popular in the group of youth to be chosen for friendship.

Now as if being a young single mother/outcast was not enough during my pregnancy, I found out information that would shatter my world and any hope I had for normalcy.

Throughout my pregnancy, I went to checkups alone and that was hard within itself. I would see happy couples all around me and I was the single young black girl in the room. I did not think there was anything more humiliating than being a walking billboard for what they consider to be a statistic within my race.

When I found out I had contracted a STD, I spoke to a few of the youth out of confidence yet again, thinking I would receive support for what I was going through. **Here is a life lesson:** Sometimes you must keep things to yourself because no matter how much you make someone vow to secrecy; there's always that one friend that tells everything to their closest friend making them promise not to say a word - and that friend has to tell her sister and her boyfriend and before you know it, people are having conversations at the dinner table about the unfortunate events of your life.

I did not understand why this would happen to me of all people or even how to get through it. My mind has always been my biggest struggle, just like many Christians out there. Assuming that I could confide in friends, became just a means in which my name and character would be beat beyond recognition and dragged through the mud.

It went from me talking to a few in total trust and confidence, assuming that I would receive support and love in one of the toughest battles of my life. These were the same people who were taking such sensitive information and trying to use it to destroy me and my character in ways I truly never thought church folks would act.

I remember some years after being diagnosed with a STD, I was talking to a friend who told me that she had been talking about this situation with her boyfriend. It was almost 4 years after I found out and I had not realized how many people knew, but I had also come to accept the result of my choice to have sex outside of marriage.

When I heard this news, my heart and any self-esteem that I had left had sunk down to the soles of my feet. I could not believe this was something I almost killed myself over and people were using it for table talk.

Among many, another incident happened when one of the same people who I was formerly very close to, knew about my situation and gossiped about it. He said something that made me feel so disgusting in my own skin - I mean I wanted to crawl into a hole and die. We were at a church function cleaning when it was stated, "I would never want to touch you in a million years."

Slinky was one of those people that had popularity just because of who he came from, so whatever he said was the funniest or most clever thing anyone had ever heard before. He was one of the pastor's kids, so he kind of had life and all the perks of ministry handed to him by default.

I never thought that being around saved folk would make me feel so worthless, inadequate, useless, disgusting and just downright good for nothing on top of the insecurities I was already living with behind closed doors.

These were some of the many battles I endured all due to the ruthless power trips of those in the saved world who could care less about what others had been through and the real issues they dealt with. Too many times we are always more willing to cast stones, than we are to cast a listening ear or shoulder for someone broken to rest on.

I had been with 'Itsy Bitsy Baptist' for about four years when I began to have desires to leave, some stronger than others.

Sometimes you just reach a point in your life when enough is enough and you are unwilling to continue enduring unnecessary hardships, afflictions and pain for no reason at all. When you know there is more - but are unable to come to a place of having it, not just watching others around you receive it.

Now we must not confuse this with the desire to become a runner. Runners are those who refuse to deal with life. Every time something happens that is not favorable or comfortable, a runner does exactly what its name describes. They run. They run from resolution. They run from work. Any relationship or thing in general that we come across in life, will require work. Runners seek to avoid maturity by running off to the next thing; seeking relief in that area or that person, never realizing that when they run, they take themselves wherever they go.

Over the years, I had become very comfortable with my Pastor Chuck who allowed me to come to him many times crying, broken and frustrated for two main reasons. The first and biggest issue I had, was not feeling as though I was being treated the way a woman of God should be treated. I did not think people should be treated the way I was treated by being used, gossiped about, never defended, protected or appreciated. There were many times I was insulted in front of large groups of people. There were times my child was told to shut up or mistreated by many of the other members my age. It never failed me to feel like I was an outsider and I did not belong. Many times (me included), we do things without realizing the severity of what we have said or done. To us it's no big deal, but to the person it is being dished out to - it's a world-shattering event. I must share this because of who I am; I will enlighten you on a song that really deals with this particular hurt.

My favorite rapper Andy Mineo, says this in his song "Still Bleeding" from his Heroes for Sale album:

"Like a car running into a brick wall
Is how your words crashed into my heart
What was so minor to you
Was so major to me
And all I wait for is words like I'm sorry. Forgive me.
I'm still bleeding." (Andy Mineo)

I also encourage you to check out his entire album if you have not already. It's all pretty relevant to our walk, no matter who you are or where you came from (that was a side note for free!). The bible tells us that: *"By this all people will know that you are my disciples, if you have love for one another"*, John 13:35 ESV. I will not sit and act as though all the time spent in the beginning stages of my saved life or with this ministry was all bad - or even that I had perfected that scripture in my own life. We had many good times with the events at the church, but isn't this so true that many times when we say things or things are said to us, the full impact of what is said is never realized? There truly is power of life and death in our tongues and we minimize that scripture. We spew out hate and love in the same breath as a means to gain laughs or with the intent to hurt, but never realize how our words affect others for seasons and even years to come and because hurt people hurt people without conviction and forgiveness, we are all left bleeding out.

My other battle I truly struggled with during most of my time there was that I felt like I had been saved too long and had not made enough progress. My personal progression in my walk with

God has been a very big mental and emotional battle I have struggled with for years now.

At one point I was very comfortable with just going to church; going through the motions and being active in a couple of the activities. I looked at other people who were not doing as much. I mean come on, I was doing it big to be a single mother and still involved with everything right? I was better than those singles that were 'lazy'. I was one of the people Christ referred to when He stated the harvest was plenty, but the laborers would be few.

After some time it really frustrated me to see people who had been 'brand spanking new' to salvation and the ministry - but had been in the pulpit and on the front row after only being in the church for much less time than I had put in. I mean these same people were CUTTING UP on Friday and Saturday night, then ministering to me on Sunday morning. I just could not understand what the heck was wrong with me. What was I doing wrong or what was I not doing, as I had been saved for longer than most, if not all of the people that were being miraculously transformed into ministers? Why was I still at a stand-still in my own walk?

I felt a great sense of uselessness in the body of Christ because I felt as though I was only good enough to do the work no one else wanted to do (not realizing that many times those are the jobs Christ truly delights in when we complete them with a proper attitude towards authority and submission). I could clean the toilets, set up speakers and sounds systems and greet people - but I was not good enough to be groomed and mentored concerning the gifts God had given me to accomplish the assignments He had just for me. I could not understand what I was doing wrong and what they were doing right that I had failed to get. This unfortunately allowed me to come to a place where my heart had become very hard towards God's people.

So naturally as a result of this I struggled with resentment, anger and bitterness for those who seemed not to be doing right, but getting much further. I struggled with feeling like those who really gave their all to God were the ones who will finish last and would never be able to receive any happiness or reward here on earth.

I had given up many of my obvious sinful ways that I knew were unpleasing to God. I had not engaged in sexual sin since the birth of my son; I did not smoke, drink or participate in things I knew would cause me to be living in a state of hypocrisy or a gray area with God. At this point I considered myself very faithful in my walk with God and the ministry I was a part of, so off and on, I had many episodes of "craziness" because I did not understand why in the world I was at a standstill. I had progressed considerably, but I still did not (in my own eyes) appear to be as successful as the people I was around (know that there is a danger that breaks God's heart when we compare ourselves to one another).

So when I had these conversations with my Pastor Chuck and addressed my concerns, I was always comforted that I had made a lot of progress and that it was just something I had a hard time seeing because we are unable to have the same view and insight as those looking from the outside in. As a good friend would say to me all the time "You can't see the parade if you are in it." For me it was even harder to see my progression because I never really had anyone to mentor me. Having a mentor on an "Elizabeth" in your life is more important than we may realize. We will discuss that in more detail later in the book.

I did not know what it was to truly abide in God or have a relationship with Him. There is a clear difference in knowing of God and truly knowing Him. I had not known it, but there was a hunger that was being stirred up in me. This hunger had manifested itself repeatedly for four years and is something I believe God allows the Holy Spirit to do inside of us continuously by His grace.

Again I had gone in and out of my Pastor Chuck's office several times during the last four years I was with the ministry with this same concern. I got my temporary emotional fixes, but there had become a time where I was fed up with everything. I was fed up with the progress I had not made, seeing others prosper beyond me that had not been saved as long as I had; watching the same people with different titles cut up, then run to the mic trying to convince me how I needed to get myself together as they were still doing their dirt behind closed doors. I was just plain old sick and tired of the rut, but not knowing how to get my head above water.

Among all the hurt, pain, shame, condemnation and embarrassment I endured while in this ministry, there was one incident in particular that hurt me beyond belief and was the very vehicle used to move me forward in my walk with God, it was something I thought honestly would only happen in the ghetto, but never in the house of God.

With being anywhere for an extended period of time, you are bound to see and experience some type of issues. Whether good or bad - there is bound to be something that will 'pop off' when you get more than one person together with many different traits, behaviors and personalities. No matter if it is work, school, sports or church - there are ups and downs as well as joys and disappointments. Many of the things I had seen and experienced while at this ministry had taken me to a certain place of insanity.

I was very thankful to God that I still had a desire to go back to church every Tuesday for prayer, Thursday for bible study and Sunday for church service without making a fool of myself.

I experienced many things that were very uncomfortable, but this was very different. This issue arose because of a young man in the church. See if you are not careful and completely alert to the schemes of the devil and the reality that he exists, you will be caught off guard when he attempts to complete his goal - which is to kill, steal and destroy. John 10:10 ESV.

Here is one piece of wisdom that I want to share with all those reading. Please take heed to this: no matter what it is you want to do in this life, if you want it to be successful, SEEK GOD FIRST. Not just for the big things, or for the things you deem worthy for God to address. SEEK GOD FIRST.

There should be nothing we will ever do without God's consent first (although this is not always how we operate as Christians). The best example of this in the Bible is David. There were times that as powerful and mighty as he was, he sought God. Many times he wanted to chop folks' heads off and just go at it with his sword - but he would choose to seek God concerning God's will for the situation, then he would act based off God's opinion of the situation. Unfortunately I had not grasped the value of this until I had reached my late twenties and honestly, not until after this particular situation.

See I have been known to be a rescuer. No matter what it was, who it was, or knowing how I was going to do it - if I set out in my heart to do something (with or without Gods approval), I was going to get it done. There were many times in my life when I would blindly walk into friendships or situations like Bambi, very innocent and naive. Having God's approval and the spirit of discernment will help to deter us from the things God would rather protect us from (but you must be willing to listen).

More often than not I had the tendency of judging the value of a relationship or friendship based on what the person looked like. With Peter Pan he was what most females would want. Looked decent, you know; tall, brown-skinned, super bulky and was physically in the church (mind you I said nothing about the state of his relationship with God or lack thereof. Any man can go to church). I mean what was not to love about him? Well soon and very soon I would see how very wrong I was.

At the point I had learned of his existence, I had been single for something like 5 years without engaging in any PHYSICAL sexual sin, so you can only imagine the excitement one would experience when seeing a somewhat decent-looking young man walking into the house of the Lord.

When I first saw him all I could think was 'good Lord Almighty', but that's all. When I truly started living for Christ with purity and holiness as my life standard, I stopped trying to make myself be seen by men. So I left it at him being one of the best looking men that had walked in that church in a long time.

Of course just like women do, I tried to snoop around a little and try to figure out where this young man had come from and if he was single. Shortly after seeing him I learned that he found interest in another young woman (well she was older than the both of us, but still considered young) at the church, so therefore I completely put any bit of interest out of my mind. At that point he was off limits. See, here's how I roll: I have never been one to be a home-wrecker. I know how long I've been single and I know how long I've desired to be married and in a healthy and loving relationship. I do respect others and marriage in general, so I would be the last person to willingly and knowingly try to destroy what someone else has waited and worked for - not to mention I was not one to be out on the Christian girl 'merry-go-round' if you know what I mean.

So as I stated, I put my interest out of sight and out of mind. Sometime after this occurred I learned that the couple broke up. Now in my mind this was not an opportunity to make anything happen for myself, seize the moment, or carry out my own agenda. See here is another piece of free advice: If there is dating going on in a small group of people DO NOT GO AFTER THE PERSON NEXT - this makes for a very messy situation, as I will share with you now!

With this young man I honestly, truly and simply wanted to reach out to him because unfortunately I had seen too many young people walk away from God (not just that particular church) due to a failed relationship. I eventually took it upon myself to reach out to him and another young woman who had been wronged in a relationship without the consent of anyone. I did not think I had to - but because I knew this young woman would think the worst, I kept this mission to myself. This would soon be a decision that I would regret with every fiber of my being. I know that we can always learn from everything we go through in life, but again through God's counsel and word, we can avoid much of the hardship and drama we tend to face on behalf of being "good people" trying to rescue someone. Sometimes God wants that person to see that through obedience to Him, they might not have gone through that hard thing or season.

So being me the rescuer that I am, I reached out to the young man without a single 'ok, yes, no, chill up my spine' or any form of confirmation from God that it was HIS WILL for me to get involved in this situation. Just like most of the things we enter into during our lives, MOST things tend to start out very well. There's that really cute and fuzzy honeymoon period when I entered into what I thought would be a very promising friendship. At first things were going very well. So well that I had the chance to get to know him pretty decently in just a few short months, or so I thought. I saw the side he wanted me to see.

It had gotten to the point where I spent a lot of time getting to know him. So much time that I was unable to see how much I had begun to neglect my relationship with God. I was talking to him for hours upon hours during the day. When I woke up he was the first person I spoke to, during work I spoke to him more than I actually worked. I mean it was so bad that many times I delayed sessions and paperwork, even ignored phone calls just to keep our conversations going. Many nights I neglected to bond with my son because I was on the phone with him. This friendship consumed me and like most people in most situations, we don't see anything wrong with it.

For a little while I really thought I just knew this dude like the back of my hand. One thing I really took pride in was that I knew his heart better than his former girlfriend. During my honeymoon phase of this friendship I was so completely and totally blinded by what I thought was genuine and true, that I never once saw the tsunami that was coming my way and fast.

One of the very first incidents blew my mind. I could not believe how ruthless and evil a person could be. At one point during this saga we were in a season of fasting. This was actually about two months after we decided to become friends. It was the beginning of the year. I was so excited about being on this fast. Now by all means I have not perfected the spiritual discipline of fasting in my life, but I had a pretty decent understanding of its importance. So I was excited and full of expectation for the New Year and all that God would be doing in my life, not realizing the drastic changes that would soon take place.

At this point no one really knew we were friends. We had only spoken on the phone and there's no way for anyone to confirm that. We never posted anything on one another's Facebook profiles to avoid light into the existence of our closeness.

During one of the evening services Peter Pan and I had been discussing thoughts of all that had taken place. We talked about the word that was given to us that night and how we all felt about it. I remember it being very awkward because at one point it had been his ex-girlfriend, Peter Pan and I in one circle. Yes, we all experienced that awkward silence of what to say next or whether we should kind of walk away slowly.

I believe it was at that point when people began to wonder what was going on. Sad to say, many had been known for participating in the merry-go-round dating scene. One would be with one for a while and then go to another and possibly back to the one they started with. Outside of that I think, or at least I thought it was 'girl code' that you don't mess with your girl's ex. Now two things with this scenario; I was not her girl (we were not close friends at all) and I was not with her ex AT ANY GIVEN TIME (emphasizing that point highly). I never once ever dated this guy. Ever.

So due to inquiring minds, a form of hurt that I've never experienced before took place and truly sent me back into a state of depression I had not felt in a long time. It was the last night of the fast and on the last night we would all get together corporately and have a meal together as we came off the fast. I had spoken to him on the way to the service. All was good.

That night we had gotten off the phone as we were approaching the building and preparing to go into the service to end the fast corporately with the rest of the church.

Again, everything was just fine and dandy. At one point I had turned around to see Peter Pan's ex-girlfriend like right in my face and if looks could kill; at that moment I would've been laid to rest. It was one of the most not-so-friendly looks I had ever seen. I began to feel tension, so I walked away knowing to watch my back. I ended up feeling very uncomfortable so I left the service early. He had known about what happened and encouraged me to stay and not let it get to me, but I had it in my mind that 'I ain't got this to do' and that attitude came over me (even right after a fast), so I went home.

I ended up being rude to the person who attempted to encourage me, with the truth of the matter as I was leaving. At home I began to feel so convicted and realized I needed to apologize. I could not go on without doing it. So I went back to the church feeling pretty small, but realizing what I needed to do. At that time while I walked down the hall, I saw that she took my absence as an opportunity to plant one of the most deadly attacks I had ever encountered.

Later that night, at one point he told me in a phone conversation there was something he had to tell me, but he knew I would be upset. Up to this point nothing he had ever said could make me upset. Actually he was very good at making me laugh. He was the goofy type. I was slightly confused as to what it was he had to say that would make me upset. Although he brought it up, he would not tell me for 'concern' of my feelings. So I kind of brushed it off as being nothing.

A few weeks after that fire died out we had a conversation. It was right before Valentine's Day. He explained to me what was said that had him in awe of his ex-girlfriend and how far she would go to hurt someone else. As I stated before, I took it very hard when I finally came to the realization that I had contracted a STD during my pregnancy. So, hard that I attempted suicide on behalf of the fear I would never be able to be with a good guy who would love me and see past this big thing in my life.

We were speaking one day on the phone and to be honest I am not quite sure how this came up, but I remember I shared that I felt comfortable with him enough to discuss this with him because for some reason, I felt he needed to know. He sat and he listened with an open ear the entire time. After I was done he then explained to me that he already knew about my situation.

I was confused because he was relatively new to the church and I had not discussed this with him before. He then proceeded to tell me that the night I saw him and his ex-talking she had shared this information with him as a warning, seeing as at some point someone thought I was interested in him. He needed to know that I had contracted this disease and needed to avoid getting into a relationship with me for his own safety.

When I heard this, I could not believe what was happening or what I had heard. I could not believe someone could stoop so low to hurt someone. What made matters worse, was that it was stated that her mother was the one who gave her the information to give to him as a warning to protect him from a woman who was disease-ridden. That I had appeared to be desperate, because I had not been (seen) in a relationship in some time and was more than willing to go after someone's 'sloppy seconds'. This situation had completely and totally brought me to a place of disbelief. Was this really happening in the church? Was this really happening to me? Could this person in leadership really be carrying themselves this way while trying to lead me?

Is this crazy enough for you yet? Well guess what - it did not stop there. Again I spent so much time on the phone with him that I could not see how he had time to really communicate with anyone else.

One night I was on the phone with him and all of a sudden he says "Hey let me call you right back". Naturally when someone says they will call back, I usually expect that they will do just that. So I waited for a little while and when I had not gotten my call, I figured I would call him to remind him of the fact he was supposed to be finishing our conversation. Before I had the chance to call him I received a text from an unknown number that truly sent me through a loop mentally. The text stated "You sneaky heifer".

Now when I saw this I was completely and totally beyond confused. There was not a single person in my life at this time that had even remotely spoken to me like this, or that I had spoken to in this manner so I was very confused as to why someone would address me like this. So I sat for a few moments and tried to figure out what the heck was going on. I picked my brain apart trying to figure out who could be sending me this message. I thought maybe it was done in error, but something told me to call the young man who had obviously forgotten to call me back. I figured he might be able to go into his phone and see if he had the number to identify the person texting me this very random and disturbing text.

Beyond my surprise, when I called him a woman picked up his phone. I was completely confused. He was a single man and lived by himself so I was very confused as to why a woman would be answering his phone. Shortly after getting over the shock I began to realize the voice I was hearing. It was that of who was supposed to be his ex-girlfriend. The very woman he had claimed he had not wanted to be around or associate with. Shortly after realizing it was her, I asked for him - only to get a very nasty response back, along with a threat that kind of shocked me knowing who she was. That was the end of that conversation.

I sat in a state of shock not really understanding what had just happened. I went from having a great day that consisted of one of our normally-great conversations, to being in the line of fire from his ex. I then found my body temp rising by the second as I tried to figure out what the heck was going on. This dude claimed they were not together, but she was answering his phone as if she ran the joint. I was just confused as to what I had gotten myself into. I was livid that he had allowed this to happen while he sat and watched her do this. He was a bit of a passive type of guy so I could totally see him just allowing her to do this and say nothing, which is what happened.

One thing about my time at this ministry and really about my life in general, is that I am not big on confrontation - especially not over a dude that wasn't mine. This drama was very new to me. I had never in my life fought over a dude before and again, not one who was not mine to begin with. While at this ministry I never stuck up for myself because I really did not know how to express myself without looking like a lunatic. At one point in my life I truly had the worst mouth and attitude of any female I had ever known; no one in my church had ever seen me go off into my bad girl stage, as I was more than capable. I mean I could truly tear you up and down the room with my words, leave you for dead and not really care about the fact that I had just dishonored God, made myself look like an unstable and emotional fool and hurt you.

At this point, it came over my mind that people really thought I was a weak link and I figured I was going to prove myself once and for all to everyone. One thing I love about God is that He has such a great capacity to love us, even in times when we can't see His covering as love and protection for ourselves. So I had spoken to someone I was very close to trying to calm myself down, but I could not shake what had happened, so I quickly got off the phone and tried to pace the floor back and forth. That only made me more and more angry, so I figured I would go back to my teenage years and punch a hole in the door. I won that scuffle, but I was still angry - so I put on my shoes and jumped in my car to settle the situation with this person in person. I had enough of all I had gone through, I was fed up with her and she would soon know just how weak she thought I was.

As I drove off, I remember going into panic attacks for the first time in my entire life. I had never been so stressed out and overwhelmed before and prior to this, I had gone through some pretty rough things. My body was shaking violently and out of control. I could hardly breathe, let alone drive. It was NOTHING, but the grace and love of God that protected me. The Holy Spirit literally drove my car that night and pulled my car over. As I sat on the side of the road not too far from my house, I called a close friend seeking counsel and comfort. For the first time in my life I was unable to properly articulate what it was that I was trying to say. All I could do was gasp for breath. I could not breathe and I could not talk. I ended up ending that conversation without being able to actually talk to the person. After that attempt to be comforted, I decided I would not go to this young woman's house that night and I sought my older brother. I had never gone to him for something like this. This had been too familiar of a place for me in a sense that I was yet again in the place of being confused as to why I reached out to someone and had been a great friend, all to be violently attacked.

I had gone to my brother seeking simply a hug. This particular brother of mine was not really one for all the sentimental moments in life or hugs and kisses - but that night he answered my call and did all he could to bring me back to reality and a sense of calmness. After talking to him and another friend briefly, I was able to go back home and remain somewhat calm.

While at home I sat on my couch and at this point it was about 1AM. I was unable to go to sleep. My body was calmer than it had been, but I was not at the place of being able to have complete control of myself or breathe normally. So I just sat on my couch trying to figure out what had happened and find my sanity as my body still went into shock every so often.

While I sat on my couch, two things happened. The first thing was that I decided to contact my Pastor Chuck through Facebook, letting him know that I wanted to address the issue. Enough was enough and he needed to address the issue. More so because it was his daughter. It was not important enough to text early in the morning, but certainly an issue that I was willing to bring light to as quickly as possible.

To my surprise he happened to be on Facebook at that time and informed me that he knew what was going on and would deal with it in his own timing. This made me livid, dumbfounded and shocked - another word that can be used to describe the perplexity that had now come over me. I had just been attacked by his daughter and I was being told he would deal with it in his own time. To be honest the first thing that came to my mind was, 'Is this guy really serious?' I had never been in a situation like this. I did not know how I wanted him to handle it, but I just knew it needed to be handled regardless and in a manner that would favor me.

Now just to add this in - this was a man who had become the second father figure in my life. I loved him with all my heart and had always looked up to him with nothing but respect and love. He had done a pretty decent job of covering me up until that point and I honestly thought he would see my innocence in this situation and cover me as the innocent one. When that did not happen as I assumed it would, I become more than frustrated. I thought it was ridiculous and unacceptable for my situation to be handled in the manner it was and I immediately began to question his authority (which is a very dangerous mindset to be in and I cannot stress that point enough).

Second, the primary source of all this drama began to call me which I found to be very interesting. He had waited some hours before he attempted to reach out to me after what happened and to be honest, I was very appalled. I mean who is stupid enough to cause and allow someone to go through this much drama and really try to act as if nothing ever happened?

My first instinct was to ignore his calls completely. I mean I was just totally astonished that he would even have the audacity to call me after what he had allowed to happen to me in spite of the fact that I had been a very great friend to him (if I don't say so myself).

I am not sure how I came to the place of even allowing myself to speak to him again, but that night some time later I allowed him the opportunity to explain his side of the story. I believe it was after some texts he sent asking for the chance, since I would not answer his phone calls.

From what he said: she had come over, he fell asleep and she went through his phone seeing our communication through texts and jumped to conclusions concerning some of the things she saw and he woke up as she was yelling at me.

That night after hearing this, I accepted his excuse. I had been around him myself when he had fallen asleep and just like most men, he is a very heavy sleeper, so I assumed he was really telling the truth. It was not until much later after this happened that we had fallen out and I questioned how does someone wake up, see someone on their phone that they bought and paid the bill for, yelling at them and not take immediate action.

Personally I get bothered (as my mom did when I was younger and even sometimes now when I do this as an adult) when my son comes up to me in the middle of a conversation and asks me who I am speaking to on the phone. I can now understand the frustration she felt when I would ask numerous times. I never took into account that this was the same phone she bought and paid the bill for.

If we are not careful, our emotions will blind us to the truth and reality of a matter and allow us to overlook very key facts of any situation or what some would call 'red flags'. This is what I did with almost everything that happened after this incident, because unfortunately, things did not stop there. There were many things that I allowed myself to endure on behalf of being a good friend and having a 'good friend' who was a master at making his mouth say anything, while his heart and mind said another.

The next day it was as if nothing had ever happened - at least concerning my friendship with him and this was something we joked about many times during the period we were friends. We always told one another that we would always be friends no matter what happened and no matter how much time had passed when we reconnected, it would be as if nothing ever happened because we had become that close with one another.

I thought that after that incident things would die down and everyone would move on to the next big thing and sadly, the next big piece of gossip never came. On top of the not-so-happy fan club I already had, his family had gotten wind of what happened and somehow, some way seemed to hold me responsible for all the negativity that was being stirred up against him as a result.

It was as if I was being held responsible for being the one that lead him into sin or caused any of the drama that had occurred. Never once did I ever see any of this coming and if for one second I did, one thing for sure is that I would have run from him as fast as I could in the complete opposite direction. I am not a fan of the spot light and with this situation I was now on everyone's radar.

The dislike from his family had really perplexed me beyond belief. Mainly because I knew his family way before our paths crossed at this church. Many times people will give clues as to who they are or what they might become, even at a young age. When I was new to salvation around the time I was about 15 years old, I was under his aunt's leadership. We had gone to the same ministry and she was head over the dance ministry I was in. At 15 years old I was not a troublemaker, especially not in the church. The church was my safe haven from the world.

I was extremely loved and liked in the church and I loved all the attention I got from those who thought I was sweet and adorable. Not once did I ever give her an inclination that I would be a trouble maker or drama starter. Now everyone has the ability to change as they get older, some for the worst and some for the better. At 15 I was not dating, so I was not one to run after guys or start drama over them or in the church in general. As a result of this I was confused as to why she had not taken my spotless past into consideration.

Nevertheless, on top of the new-found dislike from his family - I also continued to have issues with this young woman. Not only had she gone as far as to threaten me over this male (who again I HAD NOT DATED), but I was beginning to catch wind of all the gossip and rumors that were beginning to circulate as a result of my friendship with him; the perception given from his ex, her side of the story and what outsiders thought of it.

I found it interesting that people thought I was sleeping with him and was a home wrecker to say the least. It was very amusing to me to be honest. At this point I had already been abstinent (which was something that everyone knew) for 5 years after having my son and there was not a single male in the world, no matter how good he looked that would ever be able to change that outside of marriage.

I struggled with many things over the years I had been saved, but there was not a single man that I would allow to risk or jeopardize the new-found respect I had for purity and God. Of course I was not a virgin again, but it had taken me many years to come to this place of purity and peace and there was no one that was worth the peace and self-respect God had allowed me to gain. He was no exception to the rule, so when people thought I was sleeping with him it tickled me (I think that people get upset when there is truth to things being said).

Here is a quick nugget for women and men alike:

Flee from sexual immorality. Every other sin a person commits is outside the body, but the sexually immoral person sins against his own body. 1 Corinthians 6:18 ESV.

This scripture has truly spoken life to me over the years and remains the number one reason I personally refuse to have sex outside of marriage ever again. See when I began having sex, I always thought that first I was invincible as many of us do. I also thought I would be able to do my dirt and walk away from the guy without looking back, especially if I was not physically attracted to him. I thought that I was doing my thing, getting my needs met and I would never have to deal with this person ever again. You know that whole concept of 'YOLO': you only live once.

Let me be the one to shed light on this from my own personal experience: this is not true in the slightest way, shape, or form. See when we commit sexual sins:

We are allowing our souls to be connected to the person and everyone they have had sexual relations with. This in itself sets up so much drama. Have you ever wondered why you keep dating or interacting with the same type of person just in a different physical form? When we allow ourselves to be connected to someone, we have now cut off any sense of common sense we would have normally. Through soul ties we become connected and attracted to things in people that we would normally (through a clear heart and mind) stay clear of.

It affects your physical body in so many ways, such as sexually- transmitted diseases. God does not want us to experience these things, but when we walk in a lifestyle of sin we are subject to anything that may happen as a result. One of my favorite scriptures that helps me with this is: Proverbs 25:28 (ESV) *A man without self-control is like a city broken into and left without walls.* So let me break it down for you in a relative way: when we don't allow ourselves to have self-control sexually for example, we disable any and all defense against things like STDs, pregnancy, even something new I heard recently called "revenge porn". Our purity and character have no defense and no fighting chance of remaining protected from these things. Our self-control is our biggest source of defense from these things. It is the wall that protects us from these things being able to happen to and reside within our physical body.

Now let's take a look at another verse: *Or do you not know that your body is a temple of the Holy Spirit within you, whom you have from God? You are not your own, for you were bought with a price. So glorify God in your body* (1 Corinthians 19-20 ESV).

Our body is a TEMPLE (a place devoted to a special purpose) for the Lord, a place that we want (or should want) Him to dwell. He cannot and will not share that place with the soul ties we have allowed ourselves to collect over the years or however long we allow ourselves to operate in sexual sins or really any sin.

One thing that I struggled with as a result of being raised fatherless was my self-worth and value. Because I had no one to tell me how valuable I was and God made me to be. I devalued the price Christ put on me when He was hung up on the cross for my sins. I never took into consideration the unmatchable price He paid just for me. Do you remember the visa commercials where they go through a list of things: hot dogs $1.69, popcorn $2.35, DVD $9.99 time with your child PRICELESS. Now of course this is not one single commercial they ever made, but you get the point.

There are things in life that we just cannot put a price on. When Christ died in our place - the death we should have died, it was such a selfless and loving act that none of us could have ever done or can ever pay back. We were brought with that price, but we begin to devalue it every time we have sex outside of marriage or when we pour alcohol into our bodies. We strip ourselves of our God identity. We should do everything in our power to honor the sacrifice made and protect the value given through it.

That was a quick inspirational commercial! Now I believe it is much harder for people to understand something they are not in and it is much easier for people to gossip about what they would or could do about the situation and the things they do not know. Until this point the people in my church did not have a lot of juicy gossip on me to spread. They did not have a lot of motive or reason to stomp or drag my name and character through the mud. I had never given them a reason to and by all means with this incident, I was not at all trying to give anyone a reason to gossip about me. In fact, with me and this guy we had come to an agreement to hide our friendship when we were around church folk to prevent drama.

For starters, his aunt wanted him to renounce his friendship with me. She thought that I was trouble and he just needed to focus all his attention on God and not on any other relationship of any kind. Now I did agree with this, just not to the extent of us no longer being friends. When I spoke in conversation with him most of the time, we were talking about Godly things. During many days, I sat at work talking to him and we would study the bible and many times he would read a bible verse or two to me as I attempted to act as if I was working. So by all means I was all about his spiritual maturity. That was something I stated at the beginning of the friendship. No matter what, I was 110% in favor of him growing spiritually and that nothing else mattered. The year prior he had given his life to God and as a more mature Christian I knew the importance of it and did not want to stunt his growth with God. I would never ever dare do anything to stop anyone's progression in their relationship with God. I would be a fool to.

We decided we did not want anyone to find out about our friendship because he had a small idea of the impending danger of what might happen had the information gotten back to his ex. He knew her on a different level than I had, but I had been around long enough to know the full extent of what it could lead to had it gotten back to her just for her being a young black woman - although I never imagined it would get as bad as it did. Unknowingly when it did come to the spot light, it went from bad to horrible within a very short period of time. It was like one of those things that after it happens you are standing in the rubble and chaos of it all wondering: what in the world just happened.

I am not sure if it would have been any better with her knowing all along - but either way when she did find out she was not a very happy camper, which is something I believe was inevitable for who she was.

Over the course of this friendship there were many negative things that happened. Red flags for any relationship, friendship or whatever term anyone would choose to use here. At one point I had gone so far into being myself with him that during a period of time where he was unemployed - guess who paid his rent, put gas in his car, food in his fridge and helped him when he was injured? I mean I have always been a person very quick to call myself outgoing and caring. No matter what is needed, I have been and will always be willing to go above and beyond for a friend.

At one point through this all, he did lead me on to believe that something more could be birthed out of the friendship we had. I was very excited about that because first it was something I wanted (well in the sense of being in a relationship not necessarily with him) and second, because who I thought I was getting to know and who he turned out to be were two totally different people (although in reality he had given subtle warnings).

I mean he really threw me for a loop. There were times when he would post things on good ol' Facebook stating "If I had not given myself a year you'd be my……." Now I want to stop and address this very quickly. In the process of us becoming friends, as I stated before there were MANY, MANY, MANY, MANY red flags that he threw to me, but I never chose to pay attention.

I mean it was clear right in front of my face, but on behalf of the little bit of charm and game he decided to use on me, I was memorized. I mean yes he was a baby to the faith, but he truly appeared to be doing all the right things he needed to do to change and live a life pleasing to God. He was listening to worship CDs I made him, discussing scripture with me, even getting involved in different ministry activities at the church.

There was something he admitted that was so vital and I believe that had I not acted out of exaggerated hope and emotions, this would not be material for my book. At one point, he admitted that while he was in the world he would hop from relationship to relationship in pursuit of "the one". Now when he spoke of this he did it in such a way that made me feel like he deserved an award or something. He stated that he was not looking to get into a relationship after the incident, that he wanted to give himself a year and that he was proud of himself for not jumping right into a relationship after her (although he did not keep to this personal vow). Because he just sounded so darn convincing, I accepted this as him being the most mature man of God I had ever come across. A true one of a kind diamond in the rough I thought he was.

Little had I known that at this point in his life, he was still coal being processed. Now I say coal, not to be rude - but to say there is a process that takes place when coal becomes a diamond. At the point where I had attached myself to him spiritually and emotionally, he was not ready to be picked out as a diamond.

Eventually things died down a little, but at this point everyone, their child and grandmother knew about what had taken place. While walking into a bible study one day I was pulled aside by her mother, who was the Pastor Chuck's wife. She had announced to me that the situation with their daughter was addressed. That they thought what happened to me was wrong, I did not deserve it and that I needed to be apologized to.

What upset me and brought me to tears was that she spoke of this young man (who I was still friends with at this point) as though he was an animal. Well not an animal, but a term used in the Bible commonly known as a sheep dressed in wolves' clothing. It was made to be that he was the only wrong person in this (although he did play a part in all that happened) and not her daughter. When I heard these things coming out of her mouth and due to whom she was, I just sat there upset. There was not much I could say at this point. The conversation ended and I preceded to join bible study that night. He was there and could see that I was upset. He texted me and told me not to let things get to me or change my attitude.

I cannot tell you when or why, but things ended up not going too well with us. At one point I had been with two completely different women who had spoken to me about this situation without knowing about it beforehand. They both had told me that what happened was God's means of moving me forward to another ministry. Now two things about this: 1. I hate change as many do. 2. I loved this ministry and even after everything that happened I was determined that no one was going to force me out.

I considered leaving a few times, but always came back to the same thought of where to go? What ministry could match up to this one? One thing I am so thankful for is that I eventually met a few friends over the last couple of years I was with this ministry. These friends were so supportive of me in this season and were such a critical piece of my transition. My girls Laura, Keonna and Chakarian - who when I needed people to support me and make sure I was doing the right thing spiritually, these sisters of accountability held me to the highest standards.

These young women were members of a church I would later join. For me, what was cool about them and the church was that this church did not just have many youth at the church; they really invested into the youth. They did this thing at the Pastor Smile's house where one Sunday a month, we would eat lunch; discuss the Bible and fellowship. There was not a time that I could ever remember, that I was pressured about membership. I cannot remember a time where I was asked where I was from. They accepted my son and me with open arms.

Now along with these young women was one special young man. He certainly has a heart of gold; he is beyond hilarious and says just about anything he wants without regret. This young man by the name of Alex would tell me from time to time "Oh, you will be there on a Sunday morning". He always wanted me to visit his church - All Smiles Church. I always brushed it off when he said this. I was very comfortable with where I was. No matter how bad things were, it was what I had known. Even in the drama, hurt and pain, it was my safe place and I did not want to leave.

I had not known that Alex's words would come true not too much longer after he birthed them. The others at my former church doubted it. They thought I was going off mentally and going through a phase. That I would be back, but I knew at this point where I was going and that it was not just for a season, but this would be God's new direction for my life.

Beauty in Brokenness

There is not a single person that is still breathing or has died, that has not been hurt. Whether we endure hurt by the means of different people, places, circumstances or things - the fact still remains that we all have had a run-in with hurt. I quoted his lyrics before and I will add another piece of them from the same song "Still Bleeding" which states:

"And most of the time
It's caused by somebody with ya last name"

These lyrics again come from the "Heros For Sale" album by Andy Mineo. Whether it be from your family naturally or spiritually or even a friend, we all have been hurt. One thing that has truly broken my heart over the years is to watch what happens when a person becomes consumed by the hurt they endure. Not to say that some hurts are or have not been more damaging than others - but what breaks me to pieces is to see when people cannot recover.

Furthermore one thing that really breaks my heart is to see the people that have been hurt outside of the church and have gone to the church as a "safe place" or a place of hope, been disappointed on behalf of hurt and walk away from not just the church, but God as well. This even goes for the toughest and most seasoned saints.

The Webster dictionary defines hurt as being inflicted with physical pain or to cause emotional pain or anguish. This word by definition does not shine even the smallest glimpse of hope for anyone who has been hurt, to be able to bounce back from its occurrence in our lives. To me personally this does not say "Hey something good is going to come out of this", so like so many people, because of the ways we can be hurt we are often left wondering: WHY? Why me? Why them? How could they? JUST SIMPLY WHY?

As we all should, I have matured in Christ over the past 14 years that I have been saved. I have come to a much better understanding of not just the things that He can do for us and on our behalf, but more importantly, why He would do these things.

Isaiah 55:8 ESV alone blows my mind when it states: *For my thoughts are not your thoughts, neither are my ways your ways declares the Lord.* With this scripture I believe God is telling us the obvious, that we just do not think or operate in the same way that He thinks and operates - which if you think about it, is a quite amazing and comforting thing to know. If we knew in advance that we would endure hurt, pain and betrayal from those closest to us, many of us would be more than willing to ask God for a rain check on the opportunity to be used, no matter the outcome or reward to be seen in the end.

Then there is my ALL TIME FAVORITE. There is no scripture that brings more joy to my life than Romans 8:28 ESV does. Some would call it my life verse. Now this scripture just truly helps me to get through even in the times that I do not want to be brought through. See for years I just loved the scripture and the understanding that I myself, had come to concerning it. When I read this scripture, I always thought, "God is just so good for working all things together on my behalf". Isn't He amazing!!!?" But if you really dig into that scripture it is more than God just being nice enough to fix our screw-ups or the things and situations we could not control, or the mess we got ourselves into willingly that were not so great on our behalf.

Recently in my studies, the one word that I was stuck on is the word "good". The English language has changed so much over the course of human existence. That is why it is always very beneficial to look up the original meaning of a word. This scripture is in the New Testament in the Bible and originally written in Greek. When I studied this word, the Greek definition of good is "agathos" meaning; beneficial in its effect.

Now as we all know, there is nothing that looks, sounds or feels good about being hurt by anybody or anything. As I began to think of this Greek definition and relate it back to the scripture and my life experiences, it gave me a whole new insight and appreciation for God and how He operates and a new insight of Isaiah 55:8.

See God's thoughts as we know are higher than our thoughts. He and only He, knew that these things would hurt us and drive us to the brink of insanity or possibly death - but if we have even a small understanding of the love that He has for us, we will be willing to trust Him. We will trust that although we cannot see the end results, how in the world it could even possibly work out in our favor, or how it will progress and mature us into our destiny; we will simply trust that God knows what He is doing on our behalf. Through this section, I want to bring to light some things that God has done in my life as a result of every one of these hurts

I have endured. My honest prayer and purpose for sharing my life with you is the confidence that you will not just shake your head in disapproval of my pain. Trust me I went through all of this first hand so I know how terrible it sounds and how much more terrible it felt, but I want you to rejoice with me for what God has done as a result of my willingness to submit myself to Him. So are you ready for the best part of this book? Let's go!

Concerning family....

Over the course of my short life, I have seen and experienced so much hurt that honestly I do not understand how I have my sanity or the willingness to love, forgive, or even smile. I have learned that it is through all the hurt and pain we endure that allows us to come to a place of hardening our hearts and not being willing to love, forgive or smile.

We are living in a time and among a generation of so many hurt people. It is very sad and heartbreaking that so many people are now willing to hold onto hurts, which are many times birthed into grudges and more often than not, manifested in the form of senseless acts of crime.

One major thing I want to stress is that this book WAS NOT written because I wanted to get back at someone, I was bitter or wanted to expose someone's dirt. Because of each hurt, I have learned from the things I have gone through. At the time that I was going through just about everything I shared, learning was not something I was highly interested in. It is not that I do not like to learn, but I did not go into these situations thinking, "Hey what can be learned from this".

There are things I wish to share with you in hopes that someone will be set free. That as you read the bonds and chains will be broken from your heart and mind allowing you to live the abundant life Christ promised and desires for you to live. That through your willingness to forgive and move forward someone will be encouraged to do the same.

One of the first ways I came to get over all the hurt and pain was to realize HURT PEOPLE HURT PEOPLE. This is not justification for any negative or wrong behaviors. I want to make that perfectly clear, but it is at times the truth. Because of all the ways and times I was hurt, I also hurt many people. Many times I did not realize that I was lashing out on people because I was hurt - but now that I am free from this sin I can freely speak about my past habits.

For example, although I had not realized it at the time, I took my hurt and frustration out on someone who was close to this situation. The first was my mother. At the age of 27, I am a mother. I never realized the impact of some of the things I did until I became a mother myself.

I gave an example of how I did this when I was out on punishment (made to stand in the corner) and I decided to declare, "I want my dad". Now at the time it was practically true. I really did want my dad, but at that time it was being used in the sense of "I want my dad because I do not want to be around this mean woman who is doing the most by putting me on punishment. Who does she think she is?" I did these things not only thinking it would work in my favor, but I was mad at her and wanted her to clearly know it.

I remember when I dealt with this same thing with my own son. I have been a single mother since his birth, for multiple reasons. At one point, I had bought my first house and I was so excited. I was finally providing the stability he needed as a child. It was not the nicest or most expensive house in the world, but it was ours.

I had been a fan of working overtime since becoming a working adult and being a mom I figured it needed to be done in order to ensure the bills were paid. Because of the job and great supervisors I had, there were many times I was permitted to bring him to work with me, which was a life and money saver. I would work the 3rd shift because it did not mess things up too bad with our schedule. One time I will never forget. I agreed to work Friday and Saturday night shifts that needed to be filled. That Friday night I had worked getting off at 7am. I went home and gave my son strict instructions to sit and watch TV while I took a nap. He was not to touch anything, answer the door, or do anything but go to the bathroom. He always agreed with "Yes Ma'am".

A few hours later, I woke up to him coming to my bedroom begging to cuddle. Now he is six years old so it was not too much of a big deal. It is not as if he was a teenager asking to cuddle with his mommy (which we know is beyond rare). I just thought it was odd. So I told him "go back downstairs and watch TV", but he kept insisting that he spend time with me to cuddle. Something was not right. I did not know what it was, but I knew there was something off. I went downstairs to check things out. Now I will admit on my end, this next part was not the smartest thing to do by any means.

Earlier for some reason I had lit two candles in my living room, but with strict instructions for my son not to touch them for any reason and again he agreed with the usual "Yes Ma'am". When I went back downstairs I noticed a smell of light smoke in the living room, but without being able to find any visible damage, I went back upstairs. After returning to my room, I noticed my son had a visible display of panic on his face. I could not figure out what was going on, but knew I would get to the bottom of it.

I told him to go to his room and went back downstairs. When I got back to the living room, this time I noticed a thin layer of smoke in the room. Now my baby brother was a fire fighter (and just because he is my favorite baby brother) I call him for just about any and everything. I called to get his take on the thin layer of smoke now hovering in my living room. I was sitting on my couch facing the door with the front door open to air out the room. I remember turning around while on the phone and seeing a stream of smoke floating up from between my couch and loveseat. I screamed and ran over to see the piece of paper my son had lit on fire and then put under my couch. By NOTHING, but the grace of God, the only damage was very minor damage to my wood floor. I was shocked. I could not believe what he had done. My brother hearing all of this decided he was coming over and hung up the phone.

Within minutes uncle Dave was there. I called my son down and we grilled him for hours to get to the bottom of this situation. Now remember, I said things many times to my mom without realizing how hurtful they could be. He had declared that he had done it because he wanted to go live with his dad. I could not believe what was being said. You mean to tell me I have gone above and beyond for you, all for you to want to go and live with your dad?!?! The same guy who has done next to nothing for you since you have been alive?!? It hurt more than I could ever tell, but I was humbled. Later while reflecting I remember the things I had said to my own mother (who was also a single mother). I was very humbled. Now yes he was 6 at the time and I do not believe he did it out of spite. I believe he truly thought he was going to get what he wanted, as I thought when I had done the same thing - but he never realized how hurtful that would be to the one who has done all she could to make sure he was ok.

Another person and one who is (or should) be closer to me than any relative or person in this world, is my twin brother. At this point in my life, I reflect and have reflected many times and have come to an immense place of shame and heartbreak realizing what some of my childish and immature behaviors have done to our relationship.

As I shared, our dad had left us very early in life without even a memory of him. It was as if he dangled the hope for a reunion in front of me and then robbed me every single time he would declare or promise he was going to come meet us and never showed.

On top of this reoccurring hurt with me constantly, I had an overly-positive brother that kept the hope alive.

See my mom has four sons in total. My three other brothers have different dads so it was not as if they could sit and nag me about the bright possibilities or force me to have hope. Truth be told I could (and have) sat with them and trash-talked our no-good dads and it was ok. We never felt bad about anything we said. It was our own little party of negativity and hopelessness.

I never felt bad or condemned when I had them join my pity party, but with my twin brother Kendall, somehow he always had hope. To this day, I cannot understand it. It breaks my heart to realize that over the years I did not just give him a hard time with the missing fraternal covering in our life - but really I gave him a hard time with his life in general.

Instead of being a sister, I laughed at him and mocked him at times, which in reality I was laughing at and mocking his reaction or response to the hurt and pain he endured. I mean how many of us do that? How many of us are more than willing to put someone down for what we do not understand before we are willing to help them?

I guess that many times these things are bound to happen in families, but I think I did a good job at going above and beyond to make him feel less-than at times. It may have never been in front of people outside of the four walls of our home, but it was done nonetheless.

Sadly to say, today I barely have a relationship with him. I was busy being so mean at home and so spiritual at church, that I lost sight of one of the most important relationships in this entire world.

Siblings will always have a close bond, but there is not one that compares to that of a set of twins and because of my selfishness, I have missed out on that over the years all because I was hurt. All because I idolized having power over people. Not in the sense that I was a control freak, but in the sense that I knew I could break people down with my artful use of words. I knew that even if I had never fought a single person in my life, anyone could look at this self-learned talent and respect me or else they too would become a victim of my words.

One thing that I want to encourage to all readers of this book is that there is hope. It is not until death hits that we are unable to stop trying with reconciliation. God is able to do anything. No matter what it may be, He is able.

One thing I have realized over the years with family is that this is the one group of people in our lives that are hands-down the absolute hardest to prove your change to.

No matter how much you know God has done a good work in you, no matter how much you can prove to others that you are not the old person you used to be when it comes to your family - it is as if they just have a hard time letting go of what was and moving forward to what will be or what is.

I am very guilty of this myself. By nothing but the grace of God, I met my dad when I was about 23 years old. Even to this day (although I do not spend a ton of time with him) when I spend time with him I find myself always making sure he knows how hurt I was for how he left us. How I was not able to be 'daddy's little girl', how I did not have a real man to look up to, or how I truly feel as though having him in my life could have prevented me from making many of the choices I made during my teenage years.

I found myself too often making these topics come up in almost every conversation, but here is where I want to really help you. This is for all of those who know what it is like to live without both parents. No matter who was responsible for leaving I want to encourage you with what God showed me one day.

It had been a couple years since I met my dad and things had not been the greatest between us. I guess I had romanticized our reunion too much. I am thinking; I will meet him, he will fall madly in love with his baby girl, be crazy proud of all I have accomplished and all the years I never had would be restored. Well that is not quite how it all worked out.

After meeting him, it was kind of weird. I had two prior father figures in my life and they were the nicest men I had ever met in my entire life. Always smiling, very loving and very encouraging men. I just wanted to be around them all the time. With my biological father, he drank a lot and hardly ever had a conversation with me. I would go to visit and I would sit in the living room by myself. Sometimes he would put on the TV or cook something and then go up to his room. I think I tolerated this for about a year or two before I said enough was enough. I had declared that I was not about to waste my time trying to connect with a man who had not wanted to connect with me, so I stopped visiting altogether. No matter how many times my son declared he wanted to see Granddad, the answer was NO.

My mother (bless her heart) is one of those Christians that are so necessary in your life, but sometimes you just cannot stand. No matter what happened over the years my mom never once trash-talked my dad. After meeting him, I would go to her and talk about my frustrations and so many times she would say, "You need to be the bigger person", "You are the only light he sees". I am like come on lady, I AM THE KID HE LEFT. WHY IN THE WORLD DO I NEED TO BE THE "BIGGER PERSON?"

Then God humbled me through this scripture: *And he will turn the hearts of fathers to their children and the hearts of children to their fathers, lest I come and strike the land with a decree of utter destruction.* (Malachi 4:6 ESV). I do not know about you, but when I read this I was completely humbled.

Yes, I may be HIS daughter and yes I may be a whole lot younger, but as a woman and child of God with the knowledge I have - I am responsible for adhering to God's word. We cannot pick and choose the scriptures that we will abide by according to how they will make us feel.

My dad not being there, hurt me a lot. Maybe you have some family member that walked away and you are very angry, you cannot get over the hurt. You cannot let go of the past, but please let me encourage you as I have seen in my life that when we can stand on God's word in spite of how it feels, in spite of how it looks, in spite of what people say - those things make us stronger than we can ever imagine.

Our lives are not our own. No matter how much it sucks to hear or admit this, the truth still remains that when you give your life to God you are becoming a willing vessel to allow your lessons learned from hardship and pain, to become building blocks for others to use to get past their hurt and pain.

This is the reason for this book. I shared before my favorite scripture, which is Romans 8:28. In this scripture is the word good, which in the Greek means, Agathos or beneficial in its effect. Not having my dad never sounded, felt or was good for me - but now I see what my life has become as a result. I struggled with forgiveness over many years of my life, but today I can tell you I have forgiven my dad. It was through all the years of struggling with sin like unforgiveness, but having a deep desire in me for more of God that I finally came to a place of submitting both myself and my hurt to God. I was then able to come to a place of great maturity and now I am able to be in a place to firmly share my relationship with God, with my dad and so many more.

Sometimes these things happen simply because God trusts you that much. He already knows that you can handle it no matter what you are looking at or facing in your situation.

Take the story of Job as a great example:

The Lord said to Satan, *"From where have you come"?* Satan answered the Lord and said, *"From going to and fro on the earth, and walking up and down on it."* And the Lord said to Satan, *"Have you considered my servant Job, that there is none like him on the earth, a blameless and upright man, who fears God and turns away from evil?"* Job 1:7-8 ESV.

Let me make it more relevant to your situation. God has said concerning you *"Satan have you considered my son/daughter (enter your name here)? They are unlike any other. I know you can test them and they will come out of your fire as pure gold."* I believe God hand-picks these adversities in our lives for each and every single one of us. What I struggle with will not be your struggle, but the glory of this is, God knows just what you can handle. What you are responsible for doing is coming to the realization that JESUS IS ENOUGH. No matter what happens, what or who is taken away, or who walks away - JESUS IS ENOUGH. This will be one of the biggest and greats tools for evangelism God can use in your life.

If you have the chance to reconcile with someone even if late in life, return your heart to them. This is not to say allow yourself to be used or abused, but realize the grace God has showered in your life and allow someone to see you as a living testimony and walking billboard for what God can do. Our assignment is to go and become fishers of men.

Concerning relationships.....

Now on this subject alone I can write a whole book (and I plan to in the future!), but for now I will start with some of the simple things I have learned over the years.

First things first, SEEK GOD IN ALLLLLLL that you do. As you may have noticed, most of the young men that I met during the course of my seeking days, were online. Yes, I have been 'catfished' a time or two and it DID NOT feel good.

One guy I really like in the Bible was King David. There were many occasions when he wanted to act off of his rage and instead, he sought God before he did whatever it was that he wanted to do. Now let it be noted, King David did not always do things in a manner that was pleasing to God. There were times when he did some jacked up things, so all in all, he is a pretty decent example of what it looks like to do things pleasing to God and things that will not be pleasing to God.

I was a very lonely young woman in my prior days. Yes, I was saved at a rather young age, but even while in high school I did a lot of extracurricular activities. During my high school days, I participated in soccer, softball, track & field, cross-country, marching band and orchestra.

I was quite the busy kid and I loved it. I was never home and I loved that. It was as if when I got out of high school I really did not know what to do with myself. I had been accepted into Thiel College on a soccer scholarship and never went. Could never know why I made this decision, but it was made and I never went. I had even toured the college, but it just never went through. I believe that had I gone to college, I may not have had a child so early. There would not have been any time for me to make a child.

Regardless, one vital thing I have learned over the years is the need to seek God. NO matter what it is, seek God, but particularly with relationships; SEEK GOD. One of the guys I shared about was one I sought after just for his looks. I never really considered myself to be a very attractive young woman and when I saw him it was simply my mission to try and attempt to get something I never thought I was able to get. To me he looked like a model and I just knew a guy like that would never want a girl like me, so I said let me at least try.

Any other guy that I met was something that I made happen as well. There was never seeking God to see if it was His will. It was all about what Kim wanted to make me feel good. To fill the void I had inside.

At the time I had not realized it, but now that I am older I realize that we need to allow God to be enough in our lives. At one point one of my prior guys had proposed to me (over a text message) and sadly I accepted. I thank God it never went very far on my account. Even to this day I thank God I am single.

See this change did not come over night. At all. I had to fight and work very hard to come to this place. It actually happened one day when I got a phone call from my son's school. He was facing suspension (in the first grade) because of persistent problem behaviors he was exhibiting in school. At this point I was so fed up and frustrated. I did not know what to do anymore. I had spanked him, had Uncle Dave play his part, Grandma encouraged and talked to him, I put him on punishment, taken things from him. I mean you name it and I did it. Nothing was working. So I finally asked the question I believe God was waiting on for quite some time. I cried out, "God what is the problem". Again I was not ready for the answer at all and it hit me hard like a ton of bricks. I heard the Lord speak to me in my spirit saying, *"You want a husband, a real man, but I cannot trust you with your son."* Can somebody say OUCH!

It had not been the answer I was looking for or anticipating, but sadly it was very much true. I had spent all of my son's short life looking and seeking out a husband. Now let it be known I did take care of my son. He never went without in the financial sense, but spiritually and emotionally, he suffered more than I could have ever realized.

I had not dated a lot. Really at all, but when I was focused on a guy I was on the phone 24/7. I was all into the guy. Yes my child 'came first', but only in the sense of the things I did for him. When it came to the guys I was interested in, I spent hours upon hours on the phone as I shooed my son away from interrupting. I missed valuable bonding time with him over the beginning years of his life all for relationships that never worked out at all.

I would encourage all single people that whether or not you have a child you need to appreciate and become content with being single. It sounds corny and cheesy, but I am telling you the truth. I know it is hard. It took me years to come to this place, but I love it.

Without being content we are only allowing ourselves to be sucked into a never ending black hole of trying to satisfy a void that no man or woman was ever meant to fulfill.

That is one reason I believe God has not allowed me to be married just yet. See the problem is that as humans, we want to feel better, but we do not want to be better. Let me get a nice prophetic word that makes me feel good at the end of the service; but do not challenge me to change my ways. Counsel or encourage me as a friend, but only if it is going to favor how I feel about the situation.

We have to get out of that state of mind that, if it does not make us FEEL good, we want no parts in it. See, God has not called us to FEEL GOOD. He has given us a means to become more like Him and that was through His son Jesus Christ and let me tell you when He was hung on the cross for our sins He did not say, "Oh boy this feels so great". He knew the end result would be better for us. For what we will become under His submission.

So concerning relationships, if you have to even remotely question if it is a God thing - most likely it is not. Do not waste your time with it. It can drain so much life from you that you can give to others.

See with the young man from a former church I had gone to I made a few mistakes with him. I gave him so much intimacy that could have been shared with my husband. I shared countless secrets with him and invested so much time. I even went as far as to invest a nice amount of money into him that was never returned.

At one point, he ended up losing his job after he got stuck at my job driving me to work. One winter season my car was giving me trouble and as a friend, he offered to ride me to work. On the drive there (which was quite a drive to another county) I remember that somehow, some way we started holding hands AS IF we were a couple. I was into it. I had spent enough time with him that it did not seem to be too foreign or out of the blue. He had been showing signs of interest and I thought maybe - just maybe, this would really work out.

Well after dropping me off, he shortly came to tell me he was sliding on level ground and feared having to go down the hills that lead to and from my job. I invited him into my job and kept my supervisor updated on what was going on. Eventually he decided to stay. He actually stayed with me the whole weekend missing time at his own job and was eventually fired.

I felt beyond terrible. More so because he had two daughters. At that time I had set money aside from an income tax refund. I ended up giving him over $2,000 to help him maintain for the sake of himself and his girls. Whatever he needed whether it was gas or food I was making sure I did all I could to help him. All for the relationship to go nowhere. All to find out that he was talking sweet in my ear and when I left, entertaining his ex.

If we are not careful to seek God, we allow ourselves to get connected to leeches who will suck the life out of us without being able to give life in return.

I beg you, please be content being single. You cannot expect God to bring you someone great if you are not great yourself. You cannot seek to have a man fulfill you when that was never his place or ability. When you come to a place where you can soak in the fact that God is enough it brings you true joy, peace and freedom. Watch the PERFECT man of God come right after you come to this place. Trust me it feels pretty good.

Concerning Church.....

This section is the most important. If you shrug your shoulder to everything else or see no value in anything I have shared, please let this sink deep into the depths of your soul.

This is the one part of my life that after it happened I thought, "God has a plan". I had not known it, but I believe my experiences were for you. It was meant to share how the grace and love of God brought me through as He always does for us.

This was the one area of hurt in my life, which cut and hurt the deepest. I had not been prepared for what would happen or how it would be handled and there were just too many times where I sat and thought, "Does this stuff really happen in the church?" I thought maybe this happens in the ghetto, but not the church.

Sadly but true, I know there are things that have happened to others - maybe to you, that were possibly much harder to bear than what I endured.

First, I want to clarify something. Yes, you may have been hurt, but it was not God who hurt you. It may have been certain people in that ministry, it may have even been those in leadership, but God Himself was not the one who devised an evil plan or sick joke on you. It was not His plan to see just how much you could take or to "punish" you for something you may have done wrong at any given point in your life. God is a loving God. He is the author and creator of love.

Here is my proof of this:

"For I know the plans I have for you, declares the Lord, plans for welfare and not for evil, to give you a future and a hope." Jeremiah 29:11 ESV

See this tells you right here with His living word. This is all the proof you will ever need, but if you are still not convinced let me show you how I know this to be a living proof in my life.

After things went from bad to worse at the former church, oddly enough I was still determined to stay. I had been there for well over 5 years. All I could think was 'Ain't nobody gonna make me leave my church" and trust I was MORE than confident in this way of thinking. I just knew that I was going to stay and that eventually this would all blow over. It would no longer be the talk of the ministry.

To the contrary, I met two women of which one was from a hair appointment that prophesied to me. The woman (of whom I knew was a Christian woman), told me that what happened at this church was God's means of moving me forward into another ministry and that if I had not made the decision to leave that I would continue to sit. They would not use me. I would not grow.

I was beyond stunned, but I knew this was the truth. I saw newcomers spring up and become great things in the ministry, but I was still only trusted to clean the toilets. As hard as it was, I knew I needed to leave.

One thing I want to make clear is that this was a God thing. Clearly not a Kim thing. While I knew I needed to leave, it hurt beyond words. It hurt because no matter what happened or who had done it, I could never see myself having to leave my Pastor Chuck. He was one of the kindest men I had ever met in my entire life. He was a man you wanted to be around like 24/7. He smiled 99% of the time, even when things were tough. He was very funny and always gave sound advice and he was just a perfect man for the job of a Pastor in general. Over the years, I saw some other Pastors and honestly, I questioned them and their passion, but never him. He was one of the hardest working men I had ever met. When I was told I needed to leave, the second thing in my head was "I cannot leave my Pastor Chuck. Who will ever be as good as him?"

In spite of the desire to stay, I was obedient to God's call to leave and I have to say it was one the best decisions I could have ever made in my entire life.

I have seen the most maturity in all areas of my life as a result of the decision I made to be obedient and move forward. I remember when I first went to my new ministry I told my Pastor Smiles, "I know you suggest that people sit and take time to heal when they first join, but I am fine. I just want to be involved in the ministry".

I did not get too busy when I first joined, but I know my Pastor Smile's words to be true and have been beneficial in my life. Over the time I had been with the new ministry there were so many things they had done in order to make sure people did not necessarily feel better, but they were better as a result of the decisions they made to submit to the authority of God and allow Him to heal them from the inside out.

It was at this ministry where I finally learned how to submit to authority whether or not they treated me well. I remember at one point I read a book called "Under Cover" by John Bevere and suddenly everything made sense. I was able to see why I needed to respect authority figures and leaders of all types. Not because I felt like it or wanted to be a brown-noser, but because all authority belongs to and comes from God and when we disrespect them, we are disrespecting God.

After I had this revelation I was tested with this very theory on my job. I had a supervisor who I thought was after me. Truth be told, she got on my last nerve. I hated being around or even speaking to her. After reading "Under Cover", I made it my point to apologize to her. Life is never about what happens to you, it is all about how you respond to it all. The judge will not say "Oh you killed that man because he hit you? Fantastic, I believe it was justified. Let me let you go home free."

We have to think about the consequences of our actions. I believe God looks at the way we respond to the things we endure in life and I think it can reveal within us maturity or immaturity in any given area.

"Not only that, but we rejoice in our sufferings knowing that suffering produces endurance, and endurance produces character, and character produces hope, and hope does not put us to shame, because God's love has been poured into our hearts through the Holy Spirit who has been given to us" Romans 5:3-5 ESV.

I am now convinced, that everything we go through in life is meant to be a part of a character-building process for us. Who wants to learn from someone who has not had their character developed? Who wants advice or counsel from someone who does not know how to endure and press through trials in life?

I mean this can only be gained if you allow God to work in your life. You can resist and become bitter with a hardened heart and then all the things you endure are just used to stack points against people who have wronged you. You will be unforgiving as I once was and there is no way to be blessed in that. God warns us

"But if you do not forgive others their trespasses, neither will your Father forgive you your trespasses" Matthew 6:15 ESV.

This is one of those scriptures that is just clear as day. You do not need a Pastor, prophet, teacher or any person to break this down. Now there are other things in the Bible that make me scratch my head, but this is very simple. To be forgiven we need to forgive. A wise man once said "forgiveness is not for the other person, it is for you. It allows you to let yourself off the hook" and I have found this to be so true even in my own life. When I forgave people I felt free. There was no longer this heavy black cloud hanging over me. It no longer bothered me to see the person. Did you ever realize how much energy it takes to hold a grudge or be mad at someone? You have to constantly remember the offense; you have to act differently once you are around them and possibly drag others into it to be on your side. I mean come on. It takes far too much energy to be upset and unforgiving, but trust when you do it, it is so freeing.

I remember that as a result of being so bitter with people that had done me wrong, my heart became very hard. Not in the sense that it was not beating, but I was so emotionless.

I remember going to services and I always participated in worship, but when my heart was hardened I just went through the motions. People would pray for me and I would bow my head down as far as I could and give out the sound of crying. When they would try to lay me out I would fall to the ground just so that they could not see I was not really crying, but just giving off the appearance.

It was my son's Godmother who prayed for me one time after a church service. I had gone up for prayer and then as I was walking back she stopped me and prayed for me. I remember it vaguely, but what I remember clear as day was she told me I needed to stop carrying emotional debt to use against people. At the end of the prayer I remember something snapping in my chest. I believe it was on this day and as a result of my desire to be free from it all, that God answered my prayers and healed my hardened heart. It hurt, but I remember after this happened I was able to cry again and they were legit tears.

From that day on I was determined to never hold a grudge again. To forgive as Christ has forgiven, because truth be told - I am always one decision away from being the one to hurt someone as I was hurt and let me be real, real. I have hurt more people in my life than I care to share or even reflect on, so how could I ever refuse to forgive when I have always desired to be forgiven.

Conclusion......

You may be sitting and thinking I cannot move forward. I cannot forgive that person. I cannot go back to that church. Let me tell you, there are people that you and only you can touch. There are souls desperately waiting for you. Waiting for you to overcome what you have endured. God has not given us all the same story or struggles. Just like my struggle has been my mind, mouth, or forgiveness - yours may be sex, drugs or an eating disorder.

No matter what it is God has the ability to work it out for your good. Not in the sense that you will get what you want. Not in the sense that it will favor what you had in mind, but in the sense that it makes you more like Him. That when people look at you they see the Christ in you radiantly shining through all the hurt and pain.

See I do not know if you realize, but you are perfectly imperfect. You and I are very much imperfect because we have this sinful nature that wars against us every moment that we are on this earth. Some of us have it worse than others, but regardless we still have this flesh that wars against our spirit, seeking to destroy us.

We are imperfect because in spite of my story I have shared with you, I will most likely struggle from time to time with forgiving. You will still struggle from time to time, but the beauty of a struggle is that it means our fight is not over.

See our perfection comes into play when we acknowledge Christ and His power in our lives. *"But he said to me, "My grace is sufficient for you, for my power is made perfect in weakness." Therefore I will boast all the more gladly of my weakness, so that the power of Christ may rest upon me. For the sake of Christ, then,*

I am content with weakness, insults, hardships, persecutions, and calamities. For when I am weak, then I am strong." 2 Corinthians 12:10 ESV

Do you hear all the encouragement in that? We may be weak or imperfect in any given moment of calamity or hardship, but it is in those moments when we are down to nothing that our Heavenly Father gets to be at His absolute best.

Our goal is and should be to look more like Christ. We are not our own. We belong to Christ. We were brought at a high price through the most beautiful exchange any man could ever make. He cares about even the smallest matters of your heart, but you must be willing to accept that and walk in it. I believe that it breaks God's heart to know that He cares so much for us and by doing that He gave His one and only son - but in spite of this act of love many times we act as if we do not believe that He could have possibly loved us that much.

My brother or sister please let your hurt go. I know it is much easier said than done. I know it may be hard to get out of the norm, but I am begging you, let it go. As Christ has been to us let us be the same to others. Simply put, *"So whatever you wish that others would do to you, do also to them, for this is the Law and the Prophets"* Matthew 7:12 ESV.

Does this not free you? I mean in spite of the hurt you know deep down inside, you want to be forgiven if you make the wrong decision at some point, so start with others. Start forgiving so that in the event you make a wrong decision people find it easy to forgive you and it may not be all that easy, but it may not take as long.

Earlier in my book, I shared a lyric from my favorite rapper Andy Mineo. Let me share another song that happens to be very relevant to the theme of this book and my life:

"I get bitter
Kind of cold like the winter
It's hard for me to forgive
Then I remember I'm a sinner
If Jesus forgave me and washed away my sins when I didn't deserve it
Then I came forgive him (his dad)"
"Bitter" – Andy Mineo

So you say why the heck is this woman quoting this guy so much? Well I can say out of every artist I know and love, his music happens to be the stuff that gets deep down in my soul. I love his transparency. I love how relative his words are to my life. Many times, I find healing through music. Even through rap.

I remember when I first heard that song I sat with it on repeat crying for hours at work. I knew first-hand what it was like to be bitter. I knew what it was like to experience most of what he wrote in that song. Check it out. You might be blessed too.

If you have not gleaned a single thing from this book besides a new great artist, let me challenge you to evaluate your life. If there is someone in your life you need to forgive I challenge you to do it. If you need help, seek out a TRUST WORTHY friend who is more mature, a leader in your church, or anyone you know you can trust with the matters of your heart.

No matter what you do, forgive as you have been forgiven. I cannot wait to hear your story of victory!

~ Kimberly Fairley is a leader of two youth groups in her church. Kimberly loves and adores working with children and serving others. The highest honor Kim could receive in her life is to be recognized as a servant. You can connect further with her by Liking her Facebook page at: **Beauty In Brokenness** *or by sending an email to:* ***brokenbeauty116@gmail.com***

www.ingramcontent.com/pod-product-compliance
Lightning Source LLC
LaVergne TN
LVHW051504070426
835507LV00022B/2924